KEATING ON BUILDING CONTRACTS

Unive___ of Ulster

FIRST SUPPLEMENT

TO THE SEVENTH EDITION

AUSTRALIA
Law Book Co.—Sydney

CANADA and USA
Carswell—Toronto

HONG KONG
Sweet & Maxwell Asia

NEW ZEALAND
Brookers—Wellington

SINGAPORE and MALAYSIA
Sweet & Maxwell Asia
Singapore and Kuala Lumpur

KEATING ON BUILDING CONTRACTS

FIRST SUPPLEMENT
TO THE SEVENTH EDITION

BY

STEPHEN FURST,
Q.C., B.A. (Oxon),
LL.B. (Hons)
Bencher of Middle Temple

VIVIAN RAMSEY,
Q.C., M.A. (Oxon)
Bencher of Middle Temple,
Chartered Engineer, Member of
the Institution of Civil Engineers,
Special Professor, Department
of Civil Engineering, University
of Nottingham

With Commentaries on JCT Forms of Contract

BY

ADRIAN WILLIAMSON, Q.C., M.A.
of Middle Temple, Barrister

and a Commentary on the ICE Conditions of Contract

BY

JOHN UFF, Q.C.,
B.Sc.(Eng.), Ph.D., C.Eng., F.I.C.E., F.C.I.Arb.
Bencher of Gray's Inn
Fellow of the Royal Academy of Engineering
Emeritus Professor of Engineering Law, King's College, London

Original author

DONALD KEATING, Q.C., B.A., F.C.I.Arb.
of Lincoln's Inn

LONDON
SWEET & MAXWELL
2004

Published in 2004 by
Sweet & Maxwell Limited of
100 Avenue Road, London, NW3 3PF
Typeset by LBJ Typesetting Ltd
of Kingsclere
Printed in Great Britain by TJ International

No natural forests were destroyed to make this product,
only farmed timber was used and replanted

A CIP catalogue record for this book is available from the British Library

ISBN 0421 783 400

EDITOR'S ACKNOWLEDGMENT

The first draft of the Supplement was carried out by Members of Keating Chambers assisted by researchers whose names are given below. All of us have been greatly helped by the Chambers Database (a database of cases published in the Construction Law Yearbook) maintained by Finola O'Farrell Q.C., B.A. (Dunelm) and Alison Ahearn. The Editors wish to express their deepest gratitude for their help without which this Supplement could not have been produced.

PAUL DARLING Q.C.
B.A. (Oxon), BCL (Oxon)

IAN PENNICOTT Q.C.
B.A. (Hons), LL.M. (Cantab.)
Member of the Hong Kong Bar

ALEXANDER NISSEN
LL.B (Hons) (Manchester), FCIArb.

NERYS JEFFORD
M.A. (Oxon), LL.M. (Virginia)

ROBERT EVANS
M.A. (Cantab) LL.B. (Lond)
Chartered Engineer, M.I.C.E., F.C.I.Arb., M.H.K.I.E.

SARAH HANNAFORD
M.A. (Oxon)

SIMON HARGREAVES
B.A. (Oxon)

RICHARD HARDING
M.A. (Oxon)

MATTHEW HOLT
B.A. (Oxon)

Editor's Acknowledgement

RESEARCHERS:

MARC ROWLANDS
B.A. (Oxon)

VINCENT MORAN
M.A. (Cantab.)

JANE LEMON
B.A. (Oxon)

PIERS STANSFIELD
LL.B. (Bristol)

JONATHAN LEE
B.Eng. MIEE.

SIMON HUGHES
M.A. (Oxon)

ABDUL-LATEEF JINADU
M.A. (Cantab.) LL.M. (Cantab.)

ADAM CONSTABLE
M.A. (Oxon)

RICHARD COPLIN
B.A. (Oxon)

SAMUEL TOWNEND
M.A. (Cantab.)

GIDEON SCOTT HOLLAND
M.A. (Oxon)

JONATHAN SELBY
M.A. (Cantab.)

ROBERT WILLLIAMS
M.A. (Oxon), BCL (Oxon)

JESSICA STEPHENS
LL.B. (UWA)

CHARLOTTE ELLIS
B.A. (Oxon), BCL (Oxon)

PREFACE TO THE FIRST SUPPLEMENT
TO THE SEVENTH EDITION

Since April 2000 when we produced the seventh edition, there have been many developments both in the general law and particularly in the law relating to building contracts. The main aim of this supplement is, of course, to provide an update, in summary form of those developments. In certain respects, we felt that the seventh edition would benefit from a more substantial addition.

Chapter 7 considers, by reference to *Samuel Payne v. John Setchell* and *Tesco Stores v. Costain Construction Ltd* the continuing debate amongst the judges of the TCC as to the circumstances in which a contracting party owes a duty of care to the other party to the contract. A new section has been added to Chapter 15 covering Party Walls, a subject which appears to have increasing prominence. Adjudication has come a long way in terms of case law since 2000, although many of the decisions add little to the general understanding of the subject. The part of Chapter 16 which deals with Adjudication has been re-written to reflect the changes in this topic. Whilst there have been some developments in arbitration, they are more limited and a complete exposition is available in texts on the subject.

As with the main volume, Adrian Williamson and John Uff have made additions to the commentary on the current JCT and ICE forms respectively. Michael Bowsher, who is now pursuing his public and European law interests, has assisted with advice on the chapter on European law.

This supplement has been produced with generous support from those members of these chambers who produced initial drafts and carried out research. They have made the task immeasurably easier. We also thank Sweet & Maxwell for providing patient editorial assistance.

The aim has been to state the law on July 31, 2003. Limited reference to more important cases reported up to November 1, 2003 has been included at proof stage.

S.F. and V.R.
Keating Chambers
15 Essex Street
London WC2R 3AU

November 2003

HOW TO USE THIS SUPPLEMENT

This is the First Supplement to the Seventh Edition of *Keating on Building Contracts*, and has been compiled according to the structure of the Main Work.

At the beginning of each chapter of this Supplement the mini tables of contents from the Main Work have been included. Where a heading in these table of contents has been marked with the symbol ■, this indicates that there is relevant information in the Supplement to which the reader should refer.

Within each chapter, updating information is referenced to the relevant paragraph in the Main Work.

TABLE OF CONTENTS

TABLE OF CASES

(References are to paragraph numbers)

TABLE OF EUROPEAN CASES

(References are to paragraph numbers)

TABLE OF STATUTES

(References are to paragraph numbers)

TABLE OF STATUTORY INSTRUMENTS

(References are to paragraph numbers)

.

TABLE OF CIVIL PROCEDURE RULES

(SI 1998 No. 3132)

(References are to paragraph numbers)

PRACTICE DIRECTIONS

(References are to paragraph numbers)

TABLE OF EUROPEAN LEGISLATION

(References are to paragraph numbers)

EUROPEAN COMMUNITY TREATIES AND CONVENTIONS

DIRECTIVES AND REGULATIONS

TABLE OF REFERENCES TO THE JCT STANDARD FORM OF BUILDING CONTRACT (1998 ed.)

(References are to paragraph numbers)

ABBREVIATIONS

In addition to standard abbreviated references to Law Reports which may be found in such other works as Current Law Year Book, the following are used in the Main Work or Supplement:

CA	=	Court of Appeal
DC	=	Divisional Court
HL	=	House of Lords
PC	=	Privy Council
B.L.R.	=	Building Law Reports
Const.L.J.	=	Construction Law Journal
Con.L.R.	=	Construction Law Reports
Con.L.Y.B.	=	Construction Law Year Book
C.I.L.L.	=	Construction Industry Law Letter
Hals.	=	Halsbury's Laws of England
H.B.C.	=	Hudson's Building Contracts
CPR	=	Civil Procedure Rules

CROSS REFERENCES

In an appropriate context, references to a chapter or paragraph are to that chapter or paragraph in the Seventh Edition of the Main Work.

CHAPTER 1

THE NATURE OF A BUILDING CONTRACT

4. CONTRACTUAL ARRANGEMENTS

[Add as note to first paragraph]   1–17A
The JCT has now published a Major Project Form 2003 which departs from the traditional JCT Standard Form of Building Contract in a number of ways.

[Add at end of paragraph: page 6]
The Association of Consultant Architects (ACA) have produced a Standard Form of Contract for Project Partnering, PPC 2000 (Amended 2003). This form of contract is designed for use on contracts where partnering is used and includes provisions to deal with that relationship. For a case which considered the impact of partnering on contracts in the absence of such a provision, see the first instance decision in *Birse Construction Ltd v. St David Ltd (No.1)*.[26a]

[26a] [1999] B.L.R. 194 reversed on appeal on other grounds: [2000] B.L.R. 57; 70 Con. L.R. 10. See also Roe and Jenkins, *Partnering and Alliancing in Construction Projects* (Sweet & Maxwell, London, 2003).

6. DESIGN AND BUILD CONTRACTS

Suitability for purpose.
[Add to note 51: page 11]   1–24

1

Considered in *Douglas Robert Cheal v. Hale Allen* (1997) 59 Con. L.R. 106.

8. CONTRACTS WITH FINANCIAL AND OPERATING OBLIGATIONS

1–27A [Add as note to first paragraph]
The JCT now also produce a Building Contract for a Home Owner/Occupier, a Home Owner Contract for the appointment of a consultant (architect, surveyor or engineer) and a builder and a Home Repairs and Maintenance Contract.

10. DISPUTE RESOLUTION

1–30 [Insert new heading at start of paragraph]

ADR.
[Amend note 69: page 15]
CPR, 2003, r.1.4(2)(e).

CHAPTER 2

FORMATION OF CONTRACT

1. ELEMENTS OF CONTRACT

[Add to note 9: page 17]   2–01
The common law doctrine of mutual mistake and the equitable powers of
the court in cases of mistake were considered in *Great Peace Shipping v.
Tsavliris Salvage* [2003] Q.B. 679, CA. It was held that there was no
equitable jurisdiction to grant rescission for common or mutual mistake in
circumstances which fell short of those which would lead to the contract
being void at common law. As a result, *Solle v. Butcher* was not followed as
it was held to be irreconcilable with the decision of the House of Lords in
Bell v. Lever Brothers.

2. OFFER AND ACCEPTANCE

(a) Invitation to tender
[Add to note 14: page 18]   2–02

3

For other examples of offers not capable of acceptance, see also *Gerson v. Wilkinson* [2001] Q.B. 514 at 530 where the offer was "I am willing to make an outright sale for £319,000. . ." and *iSOFT Group v. Misys Holdings* [2002] EWHC 2094, Ch D.

(b) Tender

Costs of tendering.
2–05 [Add to note 25: page 19]
Goff and Jones, *The Law of Restitution* (6th ed., Sweet & Maxwell, London, 2002), Chap. 26.

(c) Letter of intent

Documents so described are frequently sent.
2–08 [Add to note 28: page 20]
For a case where acceptance of a letter of intent gave rise to a contract, see *Durabella v. Jarvis & Sons* (2001) 83 Con. L.R. 145 at 150.

(e) Standing offers

2–11 [Add to note 39: page 22]
In *Bentley Construction v. Somerfield Property* (2001) 82 Con. L.R. 163 a standing arrangement gave rise to a separate offer for each item of work which could be accepted or rejected.

(g) Unconditional acceptance

Lengthy negotiations for a contract.
2–19 [Add to note 65: page 24]
The uncertainty of the terms may reflect on the intention to create legal relations: see *Baird Textile Holdings v. Marks and Spencer* [2002] 1 All E.R. (Comm) 737.

[Add to note 68: page 25]
For cases where the manner of acceptance was not complied with, see *Jonathan Wren v. Microdec* (1999) 65 Con. L.R. 157 (acceptance by signature of both parties); *Picardi v. Cuniberti* [2002] EWHC 2923, TCC (letter to be returned signed); *Pretty Pictures v. Quixote Films* [2003] EWHC 311, QB (signature required).

2–21 [Add to note 71: page 25]
Where a letter of authority to commence is given and the parties had acted as if a formalised standard form contract had been in place, the parties may be bound by those terms: *Stent Foundations Ltd v Carrillion Construction (Contracts) Ltd (Formerly Tarmac Construction (Contracts) Ltd)* (2000) 78 Con.

L.R. 188; *Harvey Shopfitters Ltd v. ADI Ltd* (unreported, CA November 13, 2003).

Essential terms.   2–22
[Add to note 76: page 26]
For a case where the parties failed to agree upon a completion date and this was held to be essential, see *Hescorp Italia SpA v. Morrison Construction* (2000) 75 Con. L.R. 51.

"Subject to contract".   2–23
[Add to note 80: page 26]
The use of the words "to be agreed" may not prevent a concluded contract: *Mamidoil-Jetoil Greek Petroleum v. Okta Crude Oil Refinery* [2001] 2 Lloyd's Rep. 76 at 89. The words "to be finalised" may relate to questions of the formalisation of documents or the mechanics involved in the implementation of the agreement: *Global Container Lines v. State Black Sea Shipping* [1999] 1 Lloyd's Rep. 127 at 156.

[Add to note 84: page 27]
The cases in which the meaning of "subject to contract" has been displaced may be described as cases where "something has gone wrong with the language" so that the meaning can be resolved by the usual methods of construction: *Confetti Records v. Warner Music* [2003] EWHC 1274, Ch D.

[Add to note 85: page 27]
In *Jarvis v. Galliard Homes* [2000] B.L.R. 33 there was no contract because the preliminaries provided that there was no agreement until the parties entered into a deed.

Certainty of terms.
[Add to note 90: page 28]   2–24
For the effect of the words "to be agreed" on the certainty of terms and the ability of the court to supply certainty, see *Mamidoil-Jetoil Greek Petroleum v. Okta Crude Oil Refinery* [2001] 2 Lloyd's Rep. 76 at 89, CA.

[Amend note 91: page 28]   2–24
Omit reference to *Carmichael v. National Power plc*: reversed at [1999] 1 W.L.R. 2042, HL.

[Add to paragraph: page 28]
The presence of an arbitration clause may assist the Courts to hold a contract to be sufficiently certain or to be capable of being rendered so, by

indicating a commercial and contractual mechanism by which, in the absence of agreement, the parties may resolve their dispute.[91A]

[91A] *Mamidoil-Jetoil Greek Petroleum v. Okta Crude Oil Refinery* [2001] 2 Lloyd's Rep. 76 at 90, CA.

2–28 Price.
[Add to note 96: page 28]
In *ACT Construction v. E Clarke* (2002) 85 Con. L.R. 1 at 11, CA, an agreement arose out of an instruction to do work and an acceptance of that instruction although neither the scope of work nor the price were not agreed.

[Add to note 2: page 29]
In *Gillat v. Sky Television* [2001] 1 All E.R. (Comm) 461, a value of shares defined as "open market value. . . as determined by an independent chartered accountant" was not a matter which could be determined by the court.

2–29 [Add to note 4: page 29]
Mamidoil-Jetoil Greek Petroleum v. Okta Crude Oil Refinery [2001] 2 Lloyd's Rep. 76 at 90, CA.

[Add to note 7: page 29]
For a case where the contract did not have retrospective effect, see *Consarc Design v. Hutch Investment* (2002) 84 Con. L.R. 36.

Contract to negotiate.
2–30 [Add at end of paragraph: page 30]
An agreement to "attempt in good faith to resolve the dispute or claim" was not void where the parties had prescribed the precise means to reach such resolution.[10A]

[10A] *Cable & Wireless Plc v. IBM United Kingdom* [2002] EWHC 2059.

(h) Acceptance by conduct

2–33 [Add to note 16: page 30]
As to the effect of a party's reservations and the effect of communication of those reservations, see *Day Morris Associates v. Voyce* [2003] EWCA Civ 189, CA.

[Add at end of paragraph: page 31]

Where a cheque is sent on terms that presentation of the cheque shall be treated as full and final settlement of certain claims, the presentation of the cheque raised a rebuttable presumption that it was acceptance of that offer.[18A]

[18A] *IRC v. Fry* [2001] S.T.C. 1715 citing *Davy v. McLea* (1889) 22 Q.B.D. 610 at 613, CA; *Hirachand Pumanchand v. Temple* [1911] 2 K.B. 330 at 336, CA; *Stour Valley Builders v. Stuart* (1993) *The Independent*, February 9, CA; *Re Broderick* [1986] 6 N.I.J.B. 36; *Auriema v. Haigh and Ringrose* (1988) Const. L.J. 200; *Magnum Photo Supplies v. Viko New Zealand* [1999] 1 N.Z.L.R. 395.

(i) Acceptance by post, telex, fax or e-mail

[Add note at end of first sentence: page 32]   2–34A
In relation to the formation of contracts by e-mail, see Advice from the Law Commission.[23A]

[23A] *Electronic Commerce: Formal Requirements in Commercial Transactions*, December 2001 at para. 3.56.

(j) Notice of terms

[Add to note 33: page 32]   2–36
Bank of Scotland v. Etridge (No.2) [2002] 2 A.C. 773.

[Add to note 44: page 34]   2–37A
Contracts formed by estoppel
See also *Confetti Records v. Warner Music UK Ltd* [2003] EWHC 1274, Ch D.

[Add new paragraph at end of paragraph 2–37A: page 34]   2–37B
Entire Agreement. A contract may include an entire agreement clause to preclude a party to a written agreement from asserting that any promises or assurances made in the course of negotiations can be relied on as having contractual effect.[44A]

[44A] *Inntrepreneur Pub Co. v. East Crown* [2000] 2 Lloyd's Rep. 611 at 614 citing *Deepak v. Imperial Chemical Industries* [1998] 2 Lloyd's Rep. 139 affd. [1999] 1 Lloyd's Rep. 387; *McGrath v. Shah* (1987) 57 P. & C.R. 452.

3. FORMALITIES OF CONTRACT

(a) Contracts requiring writing

Contracts for the sale of land.
[Add to note 55: page 35]   2–38A

See also *Shah v. Shah* [2002] Q.B. 35, CA where an estoppel prevented a party raising a defect in attestation in a deed.

Contracts of suretyship and guarantee.

2–40 [Add to note 61: page 35]

In *Actionstrength v. International Glass Engineering* [2003] 2 W.L.R. 1060 an oral agreement of guarantee by an employer to a subcontractor to pay sums due from the contractor could not be enforced by reason of s. 4 of the Statute of Frauds 1677 and the subcontractor could not rely on an estoppel inconsistent with the statute.

4. CAPACITY OF PARTIES

(f) Contracts by local authorities

Members of local authorities and flood defence committees.

2–54 [Amend note 97: page 40]

These sections have now been repealed.

CHAPTER 3

CONSTRUCTION OF CONTRACTS

A. CONSTRUCTION OF CONTRACTS

1. EXPRESSED INTENTION

[Add to note 6: page 43]   3–02
See also *BCCI v. Ali* [2002] 1 A.C. 251 at paras 8 and 78.

(a) Extrinsic evidence—not normally admissible

Preliminary negotiations.
[Add to note 13: page 44]   3–03A
In *Aqua Design v. Kier Regional Ltd* [2003] B.L.R. 111, CA at para.12 it was
held that it was not legitimate to look at the language used by the parties in
pre-contractual negotiations as an aid to proper construction of the contract
and in *The Management Corporation Strata Title Plan No 1933 v. Liang Huat
Aluminium Ltd* [2001] B.L.R. 351 at para. 10 the majority of the Singapore

Court of Appeal affirmed that evidence of matters raised in pre-contract negotiations or the subjective intentions of parties is not admissible. At 17–18, the minority relied on evidence of matters raised in pre-contract negotiations "in order to ascertain the objective aim or purpose of the parties in relation to the eventual transaction".

But in *Canterbury Golf International Ltd v. Hideo Yoshimoto* [2001] N.Z.L.R. 532 at paras 25–27 the New Zealand Court of Appeal relied on earlier drafts of a contract in construing the final contract; the Privy Council declined to examine the law on this matter but found the provisions in the earlier draft unhelpful, in any event. In *BCCI v. Ali* [2002] 1 A.C. 251 at para. 31 Lord Nicholls referred to the decision of the Court of Appeal of New Zealand in *Canterbury Golf v. Yoshimoto* and stated that this important topic should be kept open for careful consideration on a future occasion.

Deletions from printed documents.

3–05 [Add in text after reference to note 22: page 45]
The drafting history of additions made to a standard form may be relied on in interpreting the contract clause: *BHP Petroleum Ltd v. British Steel plc* (2001) 74 Con. L.R. 63, CA.

(b) Extrinsic evidence—when admissible

Factual background.

3–08 [Add text at end of paragraph: page 45]
Background knowledge is only relevant if it is common to both parties.[28A]

[28A] *Mayor of London v. Reeves & Co* [2000] B.L.R. 211 at para.39.

Surrounding circumstances.

3–09 [Add in text after reference to note 32: page 46]
Factual matrix may include prior contracts unless it is common ground that the prior contracts were superseded by the contract being construed.[32A]

[32A] *HIH Casualty and General Insurance Ltd v. New Hampshire Insurance Co* [2001] 2 Lloyd's Rep. 161 at paras 81–84.

3–09A [Add to note 38: page 47]
But, see Lord Hoffmann's call for restraint in the interpretation of his judgment in *ICS v. West Bromwich* in *BCCI v. Ali* [2002] 1 A.C. 251 at para. 39.

[Add to note 39: page 47]

See also *BCCI v. Ali* [2002] 1 A.C. 251 affirming these principles at paras 8 and 78.

2. RULES OF CONSTRUCTION

Ordinary meaning.

[Add in text after note 68: page 50]   **3–19**

The ordinary meaning is to be determined in light of contract as a whole.[68A]

[68A] *Harbinger UK Ltd v. GE Information Services Ltd* [2001] 1 All E.R. (Comm) 166; [2000] 2 T.C.L.R. 463, CA.

Reasonable meaning.

[Add to note 74: page 51]   **3–22**

After reference to *Antaios Compania v. Salen* add *Rice v. Great Yarmouth B.C.* [2003] T.C.L.R. 1, CA.

[Add to text after note 74: page 51]

The court needs to apply business common sense and meaning to the construction of commercial documents and to avoid frustrating the reasonable expectations of businessmen.[74A]

---

[74]

Homburg Houtimport v. Agrostin Private [2003] 2 W.L.R. 711 at paras 10–12 *per* Lord Bingham, 45–46 *per* Lord Steyn, 73–76 *per* Lord Hoffman and 188 *per* Lord Millett.

[Add to note 78: page 52]

For an application of the principles in *Mannai* to a contractual termination clause, see *Ellis Tylin v. CRS Ltd* (2000) 68 Con. L.R. 137 at paras 77–85.

[Add to note 79: page 52]

See also *International Fina Services AG v. Katrina Shipping Limited* [1995] 2 Lloyd's Rep. 344 at 350 *per* Neill L.J.; *Demolition Services Ltd v. Castle Vale Housing Action Trust* (2002) 79 Con. L.R. 55 at paras 34–50. For a case where something had gone wrong because a clause had no ordinary or reasonable meaning, see *Gan Insurance Co Ltd v. Tai Ping Insurance Co Ltd (No 2)* [2001] 2 All E.R. (Comm.) 299 in particular at paras 12–25, 80 and 83–86. For a case where the clause did have a natural and ordinary meaning, see *Breadner v. Granville-Grossman* [2001] Ch. 523, paras 36–41.

[Add last sentence to text: page 52]

There are preconditions which must be satisfied before court can "re-write" a clause on the grounds that its literal meaning has no commercial purpose.[82A]

[82A] *City Alliance Ltd v. Oxford Forecasting Services* [2001] All E.R. (Comm.) 33, CA at para.13.

Contract read as a whole.

3–26 [Add to note 87: page 53]
It is necessary to look at the terms of the contract as a whole and not to focus on the meaning of a particular word: *Aqua Design v. Kier Regional Ltd* [2003] B.L.R. 111, CA.

Written words prevail.

3–27 [Add to note 91: page 53]
Homburg Houtimport v. Agrostin Private [2003] 2 W.L.R. 711; [2003] 2 All E.R. 785; [2003] 1 Lloyd's Rep. 571 at paras 11 and 183. Where terms incorporated by reference are inconsistent with terms which have been expressly agreed, the express terms prevail: *BCT Software Solutions Ltd v. Arnold Laver & Co Ltd* [2002] EWHC 1298, Ch D, at paras 42–45.

***Contra proferentem* rule.**

3–30 [Add to note 6: page 55]
The *contra proferentem* rule only applies where clause is ambiguous: *Aqua Design v. Kier Regional Ltd* [2003] B.L.R. 111 at paras 15–16 and 20, CA.

3–31 [Add to note 10: page 55]
The rationale of the *contra proferens* rule is that it protects the weaker party: *Association of British Travel Agents v. British Airways* [2000] 2 Lloyd's Rep. 209 at para. 75–76, CA.

[Add to note 13: page 55]
For a case where the *contra proferentem* rule applied to an indemnity clause drafted by the *proferens*, see *Stent Foundations v. MJ Gleeson Group Plc* [2001] B.L.R. 134 at para. 15.

[Add new paragraph to follow paragraph 3–33: page 56]

3–33A **Impact of Human Rights Act 1998 on construction of contracts.** Under section 6 of the Human Rights Act 1998, which came into force on October 2, 2000, it is unlawful for a public body to act in a way which is incompatible with a Convention right.[18A] A public body for these purposes includes a court.[18B] This may affect the construction of contracts.

Courts as public authorities. It might be argued that section 6 of the Act would oblige a court construing any contract to adopt a construction which was compatible with Convention rights. This argument was rejected in *Biggin Hill Airport Ltd v. Bromley LBC*.[18C] Although that case concerned the interpretation of a contract which was entered prior to October 2, 2000, it is thought that the court's reasoning would be equally applicable to contracts entered after that date.

Interpretation of contracts made with a public authority. In *Biggin Hill* it was accepted that it was arguable that a public authority entering into a contract prior to October 2, 2000 would nonetheless intend the contract to be compatible with Convention rights and the court treated this as part of the factual matrix (although on the facts the court found that there was no evidence that the public body had taken this factor into account when negotiating the contract). It is thought that, in the case of contracts entered into after October 2, 2000, the argument would be stronger.

It has been suggested[18D] that there should be a presumption that public authorities intended to act in accordance with their duty under section 6 of the Act in order to avoid the threat of the contract being held to be illegal and that the court should imply terms into a contract where necessary so as to allow the public body to perform its duty under section 6 of the Act.

[18A] s. 6(1) of the Human Rights Act 1998.
[18B] s. 6(3) of the Human Rights Act 1998.
[18C] *The Times*, January 9, 2001.
[18D] For a fuller discussion of these matters see *Chitty on Contracts* (26th ed., 3rd Supplement), paras. 1–024A to 1–024D.

4. IMPLIED TERMS

(a) Statutory Implication

Housing Grants, Construction and Regeneration Act 1996.
[Add to note 39: page 58]   3–36A
Gillies Ramsay Diamond v. PJW Enterprises Ltd [2003] B.L.R. 48

[Add to note 40: page 58]
The giving of factual evidence by an architect, designer or surveyor in arbitration proceedings is not within s. 104(2)(a): *Fence Gate Ltd v. James R Knowles Ltd* (2002) 84 Con. L.R. 206.

[Add to note 41: page 58]
Contracts which relate partly to construction operations and partly to other activities should be treated as severable for this purpose: *Fence Gate Ltd v. James R Knowles Ltd* (2002) 84 Con. L.R. 206.

3–36B [Add to note 50: page 59]
For the definition of "site" for purposes of s. 105(2)(c), see *ABB Zantingh v. Zedal Building Services* [2001] B.L.R. 66. For the relationship between ss. 105(1) and 105(2), see *ABB Power v. Norwest Holst* (2001) 77 Con. L.R. 21 at para.13.

[Add to note 51: page 59]
For the relationship between ss. 105(c) and (d), see *ABB Power v. Norwest Holst* (2001) 77 Con. L.R. 21 at paras 16–19.

3–36C [Add to note 52: page 59]
See SI 1998/648: The Construction Contracts (England and Wales) Exclusion Order 1998 which excludes agreements under Statute, Private Finance Initiative Contracts, Finance and Development Agreements. See *RJT Consulting Engineers v. DM Engineering* [2002] B.L.R. 217, CA; *Carillion Construction v. Devonport Royal Dockyard* [2003] B.L.R. 79 for the interpretation of s. 107(3).

3–36H [Add to text at end of paragraph: page 60]

Notice of intention to withhold payment.
Failure to issue a notice under section 111 does not preclude a party from arguing before the adjudicator whether the sum claimed was due, it merely precludes the raising of a counterclaim.[69A] A notice under section 111 must be in writing and must be served after the relevant application for payment has been made.[69B] Section 111 does not apply to payments due in consequence of an adjudicator's decision.[69C]

[69A] *SL Timber Systems Ltd v. Carillion Construction Ltd* [2001] B.L.R. 516; *C&B Concept Design v. Isobars Ltd* (2002) 82 Con LR 154 at paras.17–19 CA and *Millers Specialist Joinery Co v. Nobles Construction Ltd* (2001) CILL 1770. See now *Rupert Morgan Building Services (LLC) Ltd v. Jervis* [2003] EWCA Civ 1563, CA.

[69B] *Strathmore Building Services v. Colin Scott Grieg t/a Hestia Fire Design*, (unreported) May 18, 2000, Court of Session, Outer House.

[69C] *Construction Group Centre Ltd v. The Highland Council* [2002] B.L.R. 476 and *Solland International Ltd v. Daraydan Holdings Ltd* (2002) 83 Con. L.R. 109, at paras 30–35, *cf. David McLean Housing Ltd v. Swansea Housing Association Ltd* [2002] B.L.R. 125.

(b) Necessary Implication

(i) *Implication to make contract work*
[Correct note 89: page 63]

3–40 Reference should be to *Duke of Westminster v. Guild* [1985] 1 Q.B. 688 at 697 *et seq.*

(ii) Implication of "usual" terms—employer

3–46 [Add to note 12: page 66]

Consarc Design Ltd v. Hutch Investments Ltd (2002) 84 Con. L.R. 36 at paras
50–51.

(iii) *Implication of "usual" terms—contractor*
Workmanship.
[Add to note 31: page 69]   3–51
For considerations which affect the content of the implied term of
reasonable care and skill and the duty to warn, see *Plant Construction v.
Clive Adams (No.2)* [2000] B.L.R. 137 at 147, CA; *Aurum Investments v.
Avonforce* [2001] C.I.L.L. 1729; (2001) 78 Con. L.R. 115; [2001] 3 T.C.L.R.
21; [2001] 2 All E.R. 385.

Exclusion of warranties.
[Add to note 55: page 71]   3–55
A court may be reluctant to construe an indemnity clause as excluding a
common law right to damages for breach of warranty of quality: *The
Management Corporation Strata Title Plan No 1933 v. Liang Huat Aluminium
Ltd* [2001] B.L.R. 351 Court of Appeal of Singapore at paras 19–22; see
commentary by I.N.D. Wallace Q.C. *Singapore Court of Appeal: Two Recent
Decisions* (2001) 17 Const. L.J. 479 at 482.

5. CONSTRUCTION OF DEEDS

[Add to note 94: page 76]   3–65
For a summary of the principles of construction applicable to deeds, see
OTV Birwelco Ltd v. Technical and General Insurance Co Ltd (2002) 84 Con.
L.R. 117 at para. 14–16.

6. THE VALUE OF PREVIOUS DECISIONS

Similar contracts.
[Add to note 7: page 77]   3–67
Chiemgauer Membran v. New Millenium Experience [2001] C.I.L.L. 1741
where the court used similar clauses in other contracts as an aid to
interpretation.

B. Risk, Indemnity and Exclusion Clauses

Loss caused by negligence.
[Add to note 13 : page 78]   3–70
Stent Foundations Ltd v. MJ Gleeson Group [2001] B.L.R. 134; *Casson v.
Ostley PJ Ltd* [2003] B.L.R. 147; *Scottish & Newcastle plc v. GD Construction
(St Albans) Ltd* [2003] B.L.R. 131.

3–72 [Add to new note at end of first sentence: page 78]
BHP Petroleum Ltd v. British Steel plc (2001) 74 Con. L.R. 63 at paras 46, 47:
limitation clauses may attract a less stringent approach than exclusion
clauses but the more extreme the effects of a limitation clause the more
stringent will be the approach.

3–73 [Add to note 21: page 79]
In *CRS v. Taylor Young* [2002] B.L.R. 272 a clause requiring the contractor
to take out a joint names all risks policy was construed as excluding
contractor's liability in negligence distinguishing *James Archdale* and
Scottish Special Housing.

2. INDEMNITY CLAUSES

Subrogation.
3–76 [Add to note 37: page 80]
Caledonia North Sea Ltd v. British Telecommunications Plc [2002] B.L.R. 139.

Limitation period for liability under indemnity clauses.
3–77 [Add to note 39: page 81]
Mayor of London v. Reeves & Co [2000] B.L.R. 211 at [25] — [35].

3. EXCLUSION CLAUSES

Third parties.
3–82 [Add to note 53: page 83]
Owners of the Borvigilant v. Owners of the Romina G, The Times, July 27, 2003,
CA.

5. UNFAIR CONTRACT TERMS ACT 1977

3–83 [Add to note 68: page 85]
For cases where these provisions have been applied in a construction or
commercial context, see *Pegler v. Wang (No.1)* [2000] B.L.R. 218; *Moores v.
Yakeley Associates Ltd* (1999) 62 Con.L.R. 76, affd CA [2000] C.L.Y. 810;
Watford Electronics v. Sanderson CFL Ltd [2001] B.L.R. 143, CA; *Britvic Soft
Drinks v. Messer UK Ltd* [2002] EWCA Civ 548; *Bacardi-Martini Beverages v.
Thomas Hardy Packaging Ltd* [2002] EWCA Civ 549.

Negligence liability.
3–86 [Correct note 82: page 87]
McCullagh v. Lane Fox, The Times, December 22, 1975.

CHAPTER 4

THE RIGHT TO PAYMENT AND VARIED WORK

A. The Right to Payment

1. LUMP-SUM CONTRACTS

(a) Entire Contracts

Recovery of Money Paid
[Amend note 41: page 95]   **4–08**
Goff and Jones, *The Law of Restitution* (6th ed., Sweet & Maxwell, 2002).

(c) Non-completion

Acceptance
[Amend note 66: page 98]   **4–15**
Goff and Jones, *The Law of Restitution* (6th ed.), paras 20–047 *et seq.*

3. *QUANTUM MERUIT*

4–23 [Amend note 92: page 101]
Goff and Jones, *The Law of Restitution* (6th ed.).

4–24 [Amend note 97: page 102]
Goff and Jones, *The Law of Restitution* (6th ed.), Chap. 26.

4–24 [Add at the end of paragraph (c): page 103]
In *Stephen Donald Architects Ltd v. Christopher King*²ᵃ a claim in *quantum meruit* for architect's fees was rejected on the grounds that the architect had taken on a risk of the project not proving profitable and it was not unjust to visit upon him the consequences of that risk. The venture had been a joint effort in which the client made the property and finances available and the architect provided design services and assistance in raising finances such that both could share in the profits of the redeveloped property. The scheme did not proceed when finances were insufficient to resource the design prepared by the architect.

---

²ᵃ [2003] EWHC 1867; [2003] C.I.L.L. 2027.

4–26 Assessment of a reasonable sum.
The first four sentences of paragraph 4–26 (previously at p.86 of the 6th ed.) were cited with approval in *Serck Controls v. Drake & Scull Engineering* (2000) 73 Con. L.R. 100 at 112.

The seventh sentence ("Useful evidence. . .") of paragraph 4–26 (previously at p.86 of the 6th ed.) was cited with approval in *Weldon Plant v. Commission for New Towns* [2000] B.L.R. 496 at 502 and in *Serck Controls v. Drake & Scull Engineering* (2000) 73 Con. L.R. 100 at 112.

[Add to text after note 15: page 105]
Where there was a contractual *quantum meruit* under a letter of intent, the appropriate measure of the sum due was reasonable remuneration for executing the work not the value of the work to the other party.¹⁵ᴬ In that case, although the parties had agreed a price there was no subsequent contract because other essential terms had not been agreed. In those circumstances, the price was relevant evidence but was not a starting point to be adjusted for variations. Its most likely use would be as a check to decide whether the total value arrived at by other means was so surprising, in all the circumstances, as to cast doubt on the route by which it had been reached.

---

¹⁵ᴬ *Serck Controls v. Drake & Scull Engineering* (2000) 73 Con. L.R. 100 at 111.

[Add to note 17: page 105]
Stephen Donald Architects Ltd v. Christopher King [2003] EWHC 1867; [2003] CILL 2027.

[Add to note 16: page 105]
Serck Controls v. Drake & Scull Engineering (2000) 73 Con. L.R. 100 at 115.

[Add to text after note 16: page 105]
The site conditions and other circumstances in which the work was carried out, including the conduct of the other party, are relevant to the assessment of reasonable remuneration.[16A] The conduct of the party carrying out the work may be relevant. If the value is being assessed on a "costs plus" basis then deductions should be made for time spent in repairing or repeating defective work or for inefficient working. If the value is being assessed by reference to quantities, such matters are irrelevant to the basic valuation. A deduction should be made on either basis for defects remaining at completion because the work handed over at completion is thereby worth less.[16B]

[16A] *Serck Controls v. Drake & Scull Engineering* (2000) 73 Con. L.R. 100 at 113.
[16B] *ibid.* at 115.

[Add to note 19: page 105]
Serck Controls v. Drake & Scull Engineering (2000) 73 Con. L.R. 100 at 110. For the types of overhead which might be recovered, see *Weldon Plant v. Commission for New Towns* [2000] B.L.R. 496 at 503.

4–26A

Duties under a *Quantum Meruit*. A company working on a *quantum meruit* basis on a complex construction site cannot wholly ignore the desirability of co-operation with others at work there. There exists at least a duty not to unreasonably interfere with the carrying out of other works and an obligation to be aware of other trades' progress and, so far as consistent with the company's own legitimate commercial interests, to co-operate in efficient working practices.[1]

---

[1] *Serck Controls v. Drake & Scull Engineering* (2000) 73 Con. L.R. 100 at 128.

3. PAYMENT FOR EXTRA WORK

Recovery without written orders.
[Add to text after note 15: page 117]   4–54
If there is a valid and enforceable agreement governing the right to payment there is neither occasion nor legal justification for the law to

superimpose or impute an obligation or promise to pay a reasonable remuneration. No action can be brought for restitution while an inconsistent contractual promise subsists.[15A]

[15A] *Trimis v. Mina* (2000) T.C.L.R. 346 (NSW, CA) citing *Pavey & Matthews v. Paul* (1987) 162 C.L.R. 221 at 256.

Implied promise to pay.
4–55 [Add to note 21: page 118]
Update Constructions Pty Ltd v. Rozelle Child Care Centre Ltd (1990) 20 N.S.W.L.R. 251 at 271; *Trimis v. Mina* (2000) T.C.L.R. 346 at 357 (NSW, CA).

4. RATE OF PAYMENT

Work within the contract.
4–61 [Add to note 49: page 121]
A fair valuation will include overheads and profit: *Weldon Plant v. Commission for New Towns* [2000] B.L.R. 496 at 501 (considering cl. 52 of the ICE Conditions). An agreement to pay "all reasonable costs incurred" would include overheads and profit: *Serck Controls v. Drake & Scull Engineering* (2000) 73 Con. L.R. 100 at 110.

CHAPTER 5

EMPLOYER'S APPROVAL AND ARCHITECT'S CERTIFICATES

B. ARCHITECT'S CERTIFICATES

1. TYPES OF CERTIFICATE

Progress or interim certificates.
[Add to text after note 31: page 127]   **5–10**
The contractor may, subject to the difficulty of recovering interest as damages, also have a remedy for interest for late payment either as damages for breach of an express or implied term of the contract if the architect fails to issue certificates at the proper time or for the correct sum.[31A]

[31A] *Hiap Hong & Company v. Hong Huat Development Company Ltd* (2001) 17 Const. L.J. 530 (Singapore CA) suggests that there is no such remedy but see I.N.D. Wallace Q.C., *Singapore Court of Appeal: Two Recent Decisions* (2001) 17 Const. L.J. 479.

Final certificates.
[Add to note 41: page 128]   **5–12**
London Borough of Barking & Dagenham v. Terrapin Construction Ltd [2000] B.L.R. 479, CA.

3. RECOVERY OF PAYMENT WITHOUT CERTIFICATE

Prevention by the employer
[Add to text after note 71: page 132]   **5–21**

Whether a failure to act by the architect or the engineer will amount to a breach of contract by the employer will depend on the terms of the contract and whether the act was one carried out as agent of the employer. The duty to certify has been treated as a situation where the architect does not act as agent.[71a] It is thought that this may not be correct. In principle, the architect or engineer still acts as the agent of the employer in certifying but has an implied obligation to act fairly.[71b] Where the act is not carried out as agent then the employer will only be liable if there is a failure by the employer to co-operate. This may occur if the employer fails to call upon the architect or engineer to act where the employer knows that they are not acting in accordance with the contract.[71c]

---

[71] See *VP Developments Ltd v. Penwith District Council* (Unreported, TCC, May 21, 1999); *cf. Hiap Hong & Company v. Hong Huat Development Company Ltd* (2001) 17 Const. L.J. 530 (Singapore, CA) and I.N.D. Wallace Q.C., *Singapore Court of Appeal; Two Recent Decisions* (2001) 17 Const. L.J. 479.

[71b] See *Sutcliffe v. Thackrah* [1974] A.C. 727, HL and paragraph 13–14 of the 7th ed.

[71c] *Panamena Europa Navegacion v. Leyland* (1943) 76 Lloyd's Rep. 113, CA and [1947] A.C. 428, HL; *Perini Corporation v. Commonwealth of Australia* [1969] 2 N.S.W.R. 350 and *VP Developments Ltd v. Penwith District Council* (Unreported, TCC, May 21, 1999)

4. BINDING AND CONCLUSIVE CERTIFICATES

Definition

5–25 [Add at end of first paragraph: page 134]
A final certificate also affects liability under the Civil Liability (Contribution) Act 1978.[89A]

[89A] *Oxford University Fixed Assets Ltd v. Architects Design Partnership* (1999) 15 Const. L.J. 470.

Effect of such certificates.

5–28 [Add to note 7: page 136]
This will cover patent and latent defects. In the case of cl. 30.8.1.1 of the 1981 JCT Standard Form of Building Contract with Contractor's Design, it did not cover design defects: *London Borough of Barking & Dagenham v. Terrapin Construction Ltd* [2000] B.L.R. 479 at 486, 487, CA.

5–29 [Add new paragraphs at end of paragraph (x): page 138]

(xi) *Oxford University Fixed Assets Ltd v. Architects Design Partnership*[23A] where it was held that the final certificate under clause 30.9.1 of the Standard Form of Building Contract was an evidential bar. It precluded the claimant from being able to prove the facts necessary to establish liability, so that the contractor was not "liable" under section 1(6) of the Civil Liability (Contribution) Act 1978 and was not liable to contribute under that Act.[23B]

(xii) *London Borough of Barking & Dagenham v. Terrapin Construction Ltd*,[23C] where the Court of Appeal held that clause 30.8.1 of the 1981 JCT Standard Form of Building Contract with Contractor's Design was to be construed in the same way as clause 30.9.1 of the Standard Form of Building Contract in *Crown Estates Commissioners v. John Mowlem & Co Ltd*. The agreement of the Final Account and Final Statement was conclusive evidence of compliance with the provisions of the contract in relation to patent and latent defects. The reference to quality of material and standard of workmanship also covered compliance with statutory requirements under clause 6. Clause 30.8.1.1 did not relate to or include design defects and therefore did not apply to the contractor's breach of its obligation to complete the design of the works.

[23A] (1999) 15 Const. L.J. 470.
[23B] See the commentary on this case: I.N.D. Wallace Q.C., "RIBA/JCT Final Certificates Again" (2002) 18 Const. L.J. 1.
[23C] [2000] B.L.R. 479.

5. ATTACKING A CERTIFICATE

(b) Not properly made

Mistake by architect.
[Add to note 61: page 143]   5–38
See also *John Holland Construction & Engineering Ltd v. Majorca Products* (2000) 16 Const. L.J. 114 (Victoria SC).

(d) Effect of an arbitration clause

[Add to note 90: page 147]   5–46
Harbour and General Works Ltd v. Environmental Agency [2000] 1 All E.R. 50 at 61, CA.

CHAPTER 6

EXCUSES FOR NON-PERFORMANCE

1. INACCURATE STATEMENTS GENERALLY

Contractual term.

6–02 [Correct note 3: page 150]

The reference should be *Edgington v. Fitzmaurice* (1885) 29 Ch.D. 459, CA.

2. MISREPRESENTATION—BEFORE 1964

Fraudulent misrepresentation.

6–12 [Add to note 51 at end: page 155]

For an example where possible contributory causes provided no defence see *Morris v. Jones* [2002] C.I.L.L. 1966.

[Add text at conclusion of first sentence, immediately after reference to note 51: page 155]

If a fraudulent representation is relied upon, in the sense that the claimant would not have parted with his money if he had known the representation was false, it does not matter that the claimant also held some other negligent or irrational belief about another matter and, but for that belief, would not have parted with his money either.[51A]

51A *Standard Chartered Bank v. Pakistan Shipping Corporation (No.2)* [2003] 1 A.C. 959, HL.

[Add to note 53 at end: page 155]
Alliance & Leicester Building Society v. Edgestop Ltd [1993] 1 W.L.R. 1462 followed in *Standard Chartered Bank v. Pakistan Shipping Corporation (No.2)* [2003] 1 A.C. 959, HL.

Remedies for fraud.
[Add to note 62 at end: page 156]   6–15
See also *Clef Aquitaine SARL v. Laporte Materials (Barrow) Ltd* [2001] Q.B. 488, CA.

[Add to text at the end of paragraph 6–15: page 156]
There is no absolute rule requiring the person deceived to prove that the actual transaction into which he was induced to enter was itself loss-making. It will sometimes be possible to prove instead that a different and more favourable transaction, either with the defendant or another party, would have been entered into but for the fraud and to recover on that basis.63A

63A *Clef Aquitaine SARL v. Laporte Materials (Barrow) Ltd* [2001] Q.B. 488, CA.

4. MISREPRESENTATION ACT 1967

Section 2—Damages for misrepresentation

Section 2(1).
[Add to text at end of first sentence: page 158]   6–20
It is thought that in principle a defence of contributory negligence is available in a claim for damages under section 2(1) where the allegation is that the claimant could with reasonable care have discovered that the representation was untrue.74A

74A *Gran Gelato Ltd v. Richcliff (Group) Ltd* [1992] Ch. 560. Note such a defence is not available in the case of a fraudulent misrepresentation: *Standard Chartered Bank v. Pakistan Shipping Corporation* [2003] 1 A.C. 959, HL.

Section 3—Avoidance of provision excluding liability for misrepresentation

Generally.
[Add to note 95 at end: page 162]   6–27
However a clause in a contract, possible coupled with an entire agreement clause, could give rise to an evidential estoppel preventing the party to

whom the representation was made relying on it. Such a clause is therefore not "in substance an exclusion clause to which section 3 of the Misrepresentation Act is applicable". See *Watford Electronics Ltd v. Sanderson CFL Ltd* (2001) B.L.R. 143 at 155.

"Fair and reasonable".

6–28 [Substitute third sentence of text and note 97 with the following: page 163] Whilst it has been suggested that a term which purports to exclude liability for all forms of misrepresentation will probably be unreasonable, since it is not reasonable to exclude liability for fraud, the preferred view is that a general clause excluding liability for all forms of misrepresentation is not to be taken as covering fraud.[97]

---

[97]The suggestion, made in *Thomas Witter Ltd v. TBP Industries Ltd* [1996] 2 All E.R. 573, was not followed in *Government of Zanzibar v. British Aerospace* [2000] 1 W.L.R. 2333 and *Mowlem plc v. Newton Street Ltd* [2003] C.I.L.L. 2002.

5. COLLATERAL WARRANTY

6–30 [Add to note 2 at end: page 164] For a recent summary of the general principles regarding the recognition of assurances as collateral warranties, see *Inntrepreneur Pub Co v. East Crown Ltd* [2000] 2 Lloyd's Rep. 611 at 615.

[Add to text at the end of the paragraph: page 164] If the principal contract contains an "entire agreement" clause, it is a question of construction as to whether the clause denudes what would otherwise be a collateral warranty of any legal effect. That is the normal purpose of such a provision.[6A]

[6A] *Inntrepreneur Pub Co v. East Crown Ltd* [2000] 2 Lloyd's Rep. 611

7. FRUSTRATION AND IMPOSSIBILITY

Impossibility at time of contract.

6–37 [Correct reference at note 33: page 168] The case referred to should be *Sheikh Bros Ltd v. Ochsner* [1957] A.C. 136, PC.

8. ILLEGALITY

No assistance from the court.

6–56 [Add to footnote 16: page 176]

The Court will not permit the same relief to be obtained by framing the claim in restitution or for *quantum meruit*. See *Mohamed v. Alaga & Co* [2000] 1 W.L.R. 1815, CA, and *Awwad v. Geraghty & Co* [2001] Q.B. 570, CA.

[Amend note 17: page 176]
Mohamed v. Alaga & Co [2000] 1 W.L.R. 1815, CA.

Severance.
[Add to text at end of paragraph: page 177]   6–57
A *quantum meruit* claim for reasonable remuneration may be pursued in respect of separate services not themselves tainted by the illegality, at least where the claimant lacked knowledge of the illegality.[23A]

[23A] *Mohamed v. Alaga & Co* [2000] 1 W.L.R. 1815, CA.

9. ECONOMIC DURESS

[Add to end of text after footnote 61: page 181]   6–67
In the context of building contracts, two recent cases have stated the elements necessary to establish economic duress. In *DSND Subsea v. Petroleum Geo-Services*,[61A] it was said that there must be pressure (a) whose practical effect is that there is compulsion on, or a lack of practical choice for, the victim; (b) which is illegitimate; and (c) which is a significant cause inducing the claimant to enter into the contract. In determining whether there has been illegitimate pressure, the court takes into account a range of factors. These include whether there has been an actual or threatened breach of contract; whether the person allegedly exerting the pressure has acted in good or bad faith; whether the victim had any realistic practical alternative but to submit to the pressure; whether the victim protested at the time and whether he affirmed and sought to rely on the contract. Illegitimate pressure has to be distinguished from the rough and tumble of the pressures of normal commercial bargaining.

In considering whether there were practical alternatives other than entering into the agreement later sought to be avoided, it is relevant to take into account whether the availability of an injunction or the remedy of an adjudication were practical alternatives.[61B]

[61A] *DSND Subsea v. Petroleum Geo-Services* [2000] B.L.R. 530; *Carillion Construction Ltd v. Felix (UK) Ltd* [2001] B.L.R. 1. For a recent article on these two cases, suggesting they are difficult to reconcile with established contractual principles, see (2002) 18 Const. L.J. 2 at 87.
[61B] *Carillion Construction Ltd v. Felix (UK) Ltd* [2001] B.L.R. 1 at 9.

10. DEFAULT OF OTHER PARTY

(a) Repudiation generally

6–68 [Add to text at end of paragraph: page 182]
More recently, it has been said that there are three categories of case involving repudiatory breach: (1) those cases in which the parties have agreed either that the term is so important that any breach will justify termination or that the particular breach is so important that it will justify termination; (2) those contractors who simply walk away from their obligations thus clearly indicating an intention no longer to be bound; and (3) those cases in which the cumulative effect of the breaches which have taken place is sufficiently serious to justify the innocent party in bringing the contract to a premature end.[68A]

[68A] *Rice v. Great Yarmouth Borough Council* (2003) T.C.L.R 1 at 9, CA.

Arbitration agreements.
6–78 [Add to note 9 at end: page 187]
John Downing v. Al Tameer Establishment [2002] B.L.R. 323.

Acceptance of repudiation.
6–79 [Correct note 11: page 187]
The correct reference is *Lakshmijit v. Shermani* [1974] A.C. 605 at 616.

6–80 [Correct note 23: page 188]
The correct reference is *Bloemen (F.J.) Pty Ltd. v. Gold Coast City* [1973] A.C. 115.

6–81 [Add to text after note 26: page 188]
There is a middle ground between acceptance of repudiation and affirmation of the contract during the period when the innocent party is making up his mind what to do. If he does nothing for too long, there may come a time when the law will treat him as having affirmed. If he maintains the contract in being for the moment, whilst reserving his right to treat it as repudiated if the other contracting party persists in his repudiation, then he has not yet elected.[26A] It may be that affirmation may not be irrevocable in the case of an anticipatory breach of contract.[26B]

[26A] *Stocznia Gdanska SA v. Latvian Shipping Co* [2002] 2 Lloyd's Rep. 436, CA.
[26B] *Stocznia Gdanska SA v. Latvian Shipping Co* [2001] 1 Lloyd's Rep. 537 at 566, and [2002] 2 Lloyd's Rep. 436 at 454, CA.

Repudiation and contractual determination clauses.
6–83A [Add to end of text after footnote 42: page 190]

It has recently been said that where contractual and common law rights overlap, it would be too harsh a doctrine to regard the use of a contractual mechanism of termination as unequivocally ousting the common law mechanism, at any rate against the background of an express reservation of rights.[42A]

[42A] *Stocznia Gdanska SA v. Latvian Shipping Co* [2002] 2 Lloyd's Rep.436 at 452, CA.

(b) Repudiation by contractor

Defects.
[Add to text at the end of this paragraph: page 191]   **6–85**
An accumulation of breaches may therefore be relevant, not for its own sake, but also for what it shows about the future. Such breaches may give rise to an inference that the contractor will continue to deliver a substandard performance.[48A]

[48A] *Rice v. Great Yarmouth Borough Council* (2003) T.C.L.R 1 at 10, CA.

Delay.
[Add to text at the end of first paragraph: page 191]   **6–86**
In any event, time for completion for the purposes of determining whether a contractor is proceeding regularly and diligently is the objective time for completion, taking into account any appropriate extensions of time to which the contractor is properly entitled.[50A]

[50A] *Sindall Ltd v. Solland* (2001) 80 Con. L.R. 152 at 169.

Other breaches of contract.
[Add to text at the end of paragraph: page 192]   **6–88**
The fact that employees of a contractor company were discovered taking drugs on site in breach of safety precautions was insufficient to amount a repudiatory breach because the contractor company took it seriously, dismissed them and did not renounce its obligations under the contract. [57A]

[56A] *IJS Contractors Ltd v. Dew Construction Ltd* (2000) 85 Con. L.R. 48.

(c) Repudiation by employer

Failure to pay instalments.
[Add to note 71 at end: page 194]   **6–94**

For another factual illustration of a repudiatory breach by non-payment of instalments, see *CJ Elvin Building Services Ltd v. Noble* [2003] C.I.L.L. 1997.

No general right to suspend work.

6–96   [Add to text after note 79: page 195]
By contrast where non-payment has been found to be repudiatory, a contractor may be entitled to suspend work as the employer cannot rely on his own breach to justify a contention that the contractor is itself in repudiatory breach.[79A]

[79A] *CJ Elvin Building Services Ltd v. Noble* [2003] C.I.L.L. 1997.

(d) Party cannot rely on own wrong

6–98   [Add to note 87 at end: page 196]
See *CJ Elvin Building Services Ltd v. Noble* [2003] C.I.L.L. 1997 where the employer was unable to contend that the contractor's suspension was a repudiatory breach when it had been caused by the employer's own repudiation in failing to make payment.

[Correct note 93: page 196]
The correct reference is *Cheall v. APEX* [1983] 2 A.C. 180 at 189.

CHAPTER 7

NEGLIGENCE AND ECONOMIC LOSS

1. INTRODUCTION

[Add to note 12 at end: page 198]   **7–01**
Storey however was not followed in *Samuel Payne v. John Setchell Ltd* [2002] B.L.R. 489, TCC, in which it was held that there was no distinction to be drawn between "the designer" and "the builder" of the property and that, in so far as the designer owed any duty of care, it was a duty to avoid causing physical injury or damage to other property. *Payne* in turn was not followed in *Tesco Stores Ltd v. Costain Construction Ltd* [2003] EWHC 1487. These differences in view are considered in more detail at para. 7–31B below.

[Add to note 13 at end: page 198]
For the meaning of "assumption of responsibility" see *Phelps v. Hillingdon LBC* [2001] 2 A.C. 619, at 654, HL, per Lord Slynn: "It is not so much that responsibility is assumed as that it is recognised or imposed by law". This objective approach is considered further in *Dean v. Allin & Watts* [2001] P.N.L.R. 39, at 946–947, CA. In *Samuel Payne v. John Setchell Ltd ibid.* at para. 24, His Honour Judge Lloyd Q.C. expressed the view that "a voluntary assumption of responsibility . . . which creates a special relationship is generally not found when the parties relationship is governed by contract, especially if there is anything other than the simplest arrangement." See also paras 7–31B to 7–35 below. By contrast His Honour Judge Seymour Q.C. in *Tesco Stores Ltd v. Costain Construction Ltd* [2003] EWHC 1487 appears to conclude that such an assumption of responsibility will normally arise upon a party contracting to perform the service with reasonable skill and care.

Summary.
[Amend note 14: page 199]   **7–02**

Update the reference to *Clerk and Lindsell on Torts* to 18th ed., para.7–04 and delete the sentence starting: "The other two requirements . . ."

[Add to note 16 after the reference to *Marc Rich v. Bishop Rock*: page 199]
Phelps v. Hillingdon LBC, *ibid* at 653 and *Watson v. British Boxing Board* [2001] Q.B. 1134, at 1147–1149, CA, where the three-stage test is re-affirmed and discussed together with the assumption of responsibility approach.

[Add to note 18 at end: page 199]
Aneco Reinsurance Underwriting Ltd v. Johnson & Higgins Ltd [2002] 1 Lloyd's Rep. 157, at 181 and 185, HL. For a discussion of the relationship between the concepts of damage within the scope of the duty and remoteness, see Jane Stapleton, "Cause-In-Fact and the Scope of Liability for Consequences" (2003) 119 L.Q.R. 388 and Robert Williams, "Remoteness: Some Unexpected Mischief" (2001) 117 L.Q.R. 30.

Physical damage and economic loss.
7–03 [Amend note 22: page 200]
Update reference to *Clerk and Lindsell on Torts* to 18th ed. paras 7–84 and 7–85.

Negligence contrasted with breach of contract.
7–04 [Amend text to show note 24 after the words "nor to a third party with whom he did not contract".]

2. LIABILITY FOR PHYSICAL DAMAGE

7–07 [Add to note 35 at end: page 202]
For the meaning of "latent defects" see para. 7–05 and *Baxall Securities Ltd v. Sheard Walshaw Partnership* [2002] B.L.R. 100 at 107–110, CA, in which Steel J. held that latent defects are such defects that would not be discovered following an inspection of the nature that it might reasonably be anticipated the article would be subjected to.

[Delete note 36 and substitute the following: page 202]
In the context of a claim for nuisance concerning damage by tree roots, see *Delaware Mansions Ltd v. The City of Westminster* [2002] 1 A.C. 321, HL. The claimant was able to recover the cost of necessary repairs to its building as a consequence of damage caused by tree roots, because there was a continuing nuisance causing damage to the land itself during the period to the claimant's ownership, whether or not that nuisance caused further damage to the building during that period.

"Other property".
7–14 [Add to note 53 at end: page 205]

And see *Samuel Payne v. John Setchell Ltd* [2002] B.L.R. 498, at 511–512 in which the complex structure exception was regarded as untenable but the possibility of circumstances in which it would be unreasonable not to afford the claimant a remedy for catastrophic damage left open.

Negligent instructions.
[Amend note 60: page 206]   **7–17**
Delete: [1962] 1 W.L.R. 585 and substitute: *ibid.*

Economic loss.
[Add to note 67 after the reference to *Henderson v. Merrett Syndicates Ltd:* **7–19**
page 207]
Phelps v. Hillingdon LBC [2001] 2 A.C. 619, at 654, HL.

[Add to text, after the last sentence of the paragraph: page 208]   **7–20**
Consistently with the decision in *Baxall Securities Ltd v. Sheard Walshaw* Partnership,[72A] the defendant would argue that this was sufficient to negative a duty of care or at least break the chain of causation unless it was reasonable for the building owner not to remove the danger posed by the defect and run the risk of injury.[72B]

[72A] [2002] B.L.R. 100.
[72B] [2002] B.L.R. 100 at 110 and *Targett v. Torfaen BC* [1992] 3 All E.R. 27 at 37.

Liability for negligence of sub-contractors.
[Add to note 83 at end: page 210]   **7–23A**
For a review of the position .in various common law jurisdictions, see Christudason and Netto "Of Delegable and Non-Delegable Duties in the Construction Industry" (2000) 16 Const. L.J. 88.

[Add to note 84 at end: page 210]
It is thought that similarly if a contractor has assumed responsibility to the claimant for the supervision of the sub-contractor's work, he may also be liable if he ought to have detected and warned that the work was being carried out defectively or dangerously.

3. OTHER CATEGORIES OF NEGLIGENCE

[Add note 96A after "(3) the incremental approach": page 211]   **7–25**

[96A] See also *McLoughlin v. Grovers* [2002] P.N.L.R. 21, at 525, CA, identifying four tests of a "battery of tests which the House of Lords has taught us to use".

Assuming responsibility.
[Add to note 10 at end: page 213]   **7–30**

cf. Merrett v. Babb [2001] Q.B. 1174, at 1194, CA, where an employed valuer who knew the claimant would rely on his skill and care, signed the valuation report and was a person competent to value for the purposes of s. 13 of the Building Societies Act 1986 was held to have assumed personal responsibility for the valuation.

7–31 [Add to note 11 at end: page 214]
See also *Phelps v. Hillingdon LBC* [2001] 2 A.C. 619, at 654, HL; *Watson v. British Boxing Board* [2001] Q.B. 1134.

7–31B [Amend note 17: page 215]
Storey v. Charles Church Developments Ltd 73 Con. L.R. 1

[Delete text after the sentence starting "On this basis the judge held that . . .", followed by the quotation from *Storey* ending with the words ". . ..contractual obligations" and substitute the following: page 216]

In *Samuel Payne v. John Setchell Ltd*[20A] civil engineers were instructed to carry out a ground investigation of a site and existing foundations in connection with the extension of a cottage. Acting on their advice the claimant demolished the cottage and constructed two new cottages on structural raft foundations. The engineers prepared structural drawings, inspected the foundations and reinforcement and certified that the works had been carried out to their satisfaction. Subsequently the same engineers were engaged in connection with the construction of further cottages and in this case the engineers inspected the ground and foundations and provided certification. The judge concluded, relying on *Murphy and DOE v. Bates*,[20B] that "as a matter of policy, although a builder must be taken to have foreseen the possibility of loss or damage arising from inherently defective work for which it was responsible, it did not owe a duty of care to anybody (including the person who engaged the builder) to avoid causing such loss or damage unless it was physical injury to persons or damage to property other than the building itself."[20C] He further concluded that a "builder" for these purposes encompasses "whoever was primarily responsible for the defect"[20D] and therefore covered the engineers in this case. Whilst the judge accepted that liability could arise as a result of reliance on advice or statements, where there is in law an assumption of responsibility for loss, such an assumption of responsibility "is generally not found when the parties' relationship is governed by contract, especially if there is anything other than the simplest arrangement."[20E] The judge therefore disagreed with the both the reasoning and conclusion in *Storey*.

In *Tesco Stores v. Costain Construction Ltd*[20F] the store owner sought to recover for losses arising out of a fire. The judge, having considered the decisions referred to above disagreed with the approach taken in *Samuel Payne*. In particular he concluded that ". . .anyone who undertakes by contract to perform a service for another upon terms, express or implied, that the service will be performed with reasonable skill and care, owes a duty of care to like effect to the other contracting party or parties which extends to not causing economic loss, there seems to be no logical justification for making an exception in the case of a builder or the designer of a building."[20G] He thus held that the builder owed the store owner a duty of care in respect of the work which it carried out (as opposed to its sub-contractor) which duty included not causing economic loss.

In the light of this disagreement between judges of the TCC it is impossible to be confident as to the present state of the law. The central disagreement centres on the extent to which (if at all) the making of a contract in itself gives rise to an assumption of responsibility within the meaning of *Henderson v. Merrett (No.1)*. It is difficult to disagree with the view that a contract which stipulates that the contracting party will perform certain services involves an assumption of responsibility which will normally be relied upon by the other contracting party. On the other hand it is true that the authorities prior to *Henderson v. Merrett (No.1)*, and in particular *Murphy*, did not envisage a builder (or possibly a builder-designer or a pure designer and supervisor of work) owing duties of care in respect of economic loss. This difference of view requires a reconciliation of these two different streams of authority which will have to await a decision from the Court of Appeal or the House of Lords.

20A [2002] B.L.R. 489.
20B [1991] 1 A.C. 398, HL.
20C [2001] B.L.R. 489 at para. 28.
20D *ibid*. at para. 30.
20E *ibid*. at para. 24.
20F [2003] EWHC 1487.
20G *ibid*. para. 230.

Contractual influences.
[Amend note 29: page 217]   7–34A
Amend the reference for *Henderson v. Merrett* to [1995] 2 A.C. 145.
Amend the reference for *Storey v. Charles Church* to 73 Con. L.R. 1.

[Add to note 29 at end: page 217]
Cf. Samuel Payne v. John Setchell Ltd [2002] B.L.R. 489.

[Add to note 38 after the reference to *Norwich City Council v. Harvey*: page 219]   7–35
R M Turton & Co Ltd v. Kerslake and Partners [2000] 3 N.Z.L.R. 406.

Professional negligence.
[Add new text at end of paragraph: page 221]   7–38
In *Samuel Payne v. John Setchell Ltd*,[48A] His Honour Judge Lloyd Q.C.

reached such a conclusion but on the basis that both the designer and contractor were a "builder" who owed no duty not to cause economic loss.

---

⁴⁸ᴬ [2002] B.L.R. 489.

(a) Negligent misstatement

Possible circumstances discussed.
7–47 [Add to note 79 at end: page 225]
Cf. R M Turton & Co Ltd v. Kerslake and Partners [2000] 3 N.Z.L.R. 406, New Zealand Court of Appeal, Thomas J. dissenting.

Contractor's duty to warn.
7–49 [Add to note 86 at end: page 226]
Aurum Investments Ltd v. Avonforce (2001) 78 Con. L.R. 115.

Consultants.
7–53 [Add to note 3 at end: page 228]
Storey v. Charles Church was itself not followed in *Samuel Payne v. John Setchell Ltd* as discussed at para. 7–31B above.

Building society valuations.
7–55 [Add to note 10 after the reference to *McCullagh v. Lane Fox*: page 229]
The Governor and Company of the Bank of Scotland v. Fuller Peiser [2002] P.N.L.R. 13.

[Add to note 10 at end: page 229]
For the personal liability of an employed surveyor, see *Merrett v. Babb* [2001] Q.B. 1174.

Disclaimer.
7–59 [Add to note 25 at end: page 231]
See also *The Governor and Company of the Bank of Scotland v. Fuller Peiser* [2002] P.N.L.R. 13.

CHAPTER 8

DEFAULT OF THE PARTIES—DAMAGES

1. PRINCIPLES UPON WHICH DAMAGES ARE AWARDED

Damages for breach of contract.
[Add to note 9 at end: page 235]   **8–03**
Attorney General v. Blake [2001] 1 A.C. 268, HL.

Date of assessment.
[Amend note 36: page 239]   **8–12**
Delete *"Alcoa Minerals of Jamaica Inc. v. Herbert Broderick* [2000] B.L.R. 729,
PC" and insert *"Alcoa Minerals of Jamaica Inc. v. Herbert Broderick* [2002] 1
AC 371, PC".

[Amend note 45A: page 240]   **8–14**
Update the reference to [2002] 1 A.C. 371 at 383, PC.

Mitigation of loss.
[Amend note 49: page 241]   **8–16**
After the reference to *Sotios Shipping v. Sameiet Solholt*, add *Geest plc v.
Lansiquot* [2002] 1 W.L.R. 3111, PC; *Saunders v. Williams* [2003] B.L.R. 125.

[Note 53: page 241]
Amend the reference for *Sealace Shipping v. Oceanvoice Shipping* to [1991] 1
Lloyd's Rep. 120 and add *Voaden v. Champion (The "Baltic Surveyor")*
[2002] 1 Lloyd's Rep. 623.

2. CAUSATION AND CONCURRENT CAUSES

Causation generally.
[Amend note 56: page 242]   **8–18**

Add at end: *Fairchild v. Glenhaven Funeral Services Ltd* [2003] 1 A.C. 32, HL; *Chester v. Afshar* [2003] Q.B. 356, CA.

Update the reference to *Blue Circle Industries Ltd v. Ministry of Defence* to [1999] Ch. 289.

[Add at end of note 57: page 242]
Horton v. Taplin Contracts Ltd [2003] B.L.R. 74.

[Amend note 59: page 242]
This decision (on the recoverability of damages for the birth of an unwanted child) was overruled in *McFarlane v. Tayside Health Board* [2000] 2 A.C. 59 but the proposition in the text is still thought to be good law. See, for example, *Vinmar International Ltd v. Theresa Navigation SA* [2001] 2 Lloyd's Rep. 1, at 11.

[Add at end of note 62: page 242]
See also *HOK Sport v. Aintree Racecourse Company Ltd* [2003] B.L.R. 155.

Contributory negligence.
8–19 [Amend note 65: page 243]
Update reference to *Platform Home Loans Ltd v. Oyston Shipways Ltd* to [2000] 2 A.C. 190, HL.

Add at end: *Reeves v. Commissioner of Police of the Metropolis* [2000] A.C. 360, HL.

[Note 72: page 243]
Add after the reference to *Alliance & Leicester Building Society v. Edgestop*: see also *Standard Chartered Bank v. Pakistan National Shipping Corporation* [2003] 1 A.C. 959, HL in which it was held that a defence of contributory negligence was not available where the claimant had parted with his money because of the defendant's deceit but also some negligent belief on his part.

Statutory contribution.
8–20 [Add to text after the first sentence: page 243]
The concept of "the same damage" has given rise to some difficulty. The words are to be applied without gloss to the proper evaluation and comparison of the claims alleged to qualify for contribution. Thus "the same damage" does not mean substantially or materially similar damage.[73A]

[73A] *Royal Brompton Hospital NHS Trust v. Hammond (No.3)* [2002] 1 W.L.R. 1397 at 1410, HL. Cases decided on this point prior to this decision are either overruled or to be read with caution: see *Friends Provident Life Office v. Hillier Parker May & Rowden* [1997] Q.B. 85, *Bovis Construction Ltd. v. Commercial Union Assurance Co. plc* [2001] 1 Lloyd's Rep. 416,

Hurstwood Developments Ltd v. Motor and General & Andersley & Co Insurance Services Ltd [2001] EWCA Civ 1785, *Bovis Lend Lease Ltd v. Saillard Fuller & Partners* (2001) 77 Con. L.R. 134 and *Howkins & Harrison v. Tyler* [2001] Lloyd's Rep. P.N. 1, CA.

[Amend note 75: page 244]
Update reference to *Oxford University Fixed Assets v. Architects Design Partnership* to (1999) 64 Con. L.R. 12.
Add: *Cooperative Retail Services Ltd. v. Taylor Young Partnership Ltd.* [2002] 1 W.L.R. 1419.

(a) Concurrent causes—tort

[Add to note 79 at end: page 244]   8–21
Fairchild v. Glenhaven Funeral Services Ltd. [2003] 1 A.C. 32, HL.

The law unclear—discussion.
[Add to note 89: page 246]   8–26
See, for example, *Brownsville Holdings Ltd. v. Adamjee Insurance Co. Ltd.* ("*The Milasan*") [2000] 2 Lloyd's Rep. 458 at paras 19–20.

[Add to note 97: page 248]   8–31
See also *Henry Boot Construction (UK) Ltd v. Malmaison Hotel (Manchester) Ltd* [1999] Con. L.R. 32 and *Royal Brompton Hospital NHS Trust v. Hammond (No. 7)* [2001] 76 Con. L.R. 148. This part of the text, the decision in *H Fairweather v. London Borough of Wandsworth* and these cases are discussed by John Marrin Q.C. in *Concurrent Delay* (2002) 18 Const. L.J. 436. Although doubts are expressed about the dominant cause approach, it is thought that this is in the context of the contractor's rights to extensions of time rather than causation generally.

3. VARIOUS GENERAL CONSIDERATIONS

Contingency.
[Add to note 12 at end: page 250]   8–35
A loss of a chance may itself constitute a head of loss where the provision of the chance was the very object of the duty breached. See cases at note 9; *Allied Maples Group Ltd. v. Simmons & Simmons* [1995] 1 W.L.R. 1602, CA.

Loss of profits and loss of good will.
[Add to note 21 at end: page 251]   8–36
There may be such an award at least where the claimant has a legitimate interest in preventing the defendant's profit-making activity and otherwise suffers no financial loss: *Attorney General v. Blake* [2001] 1 A.C. 268 at 285; also *Experience Hendrix v. PPX Enterprises Inc.* [2003] C.I.L.L. 1985. However it is difficult to envisage such circumstances arising in connection with a building contract.

Third-party losses.

8–40 [Note 30: page 252]
Add after reference to *Prudential Assurance v. Newman Industries*: *Johnson v. Gore Wood & Co. (No.1)* [2002] 2 A.C. 1, HL.

[Note 32: page 252]
Update reference to *Alfred McAlpine v. Panatown (No.1)* to [2001] 1 A.C. 518, HL.

[Add to note 34 at end: page 252]
If a company and shareholder can both sue to recover loss, neither may recover loss caused to the other *Johnson v. Gore Wood* [2002] 1 A.C. 1 at 35, HL.

Cost of reports.

8–41 [Add to note 35 at end: page 253]
For similar "recovery" services in relation to salvage claims, see *Papera Traders Co. Ltd v. Hyundai Merchant Marine Co. Ltd (The "Eurasian Dream") (No. 2)* [2002] 2 Lloyd's Rep. 692.

[Add to note 37 at end: page 253]
See also *Admiral Management Services Ltd v. Para Protect Europe Ltd* [2002] 1 W.L.R. 2722. In *Amec Process and Energy Ltd v. Stork Engineers & Contractors BV* (unreported) March 15, 2002, it was held that the costs incurred by the claimant's own personnel and agency staff in collating, analysing, presenting and supporting evidence was in principle recoverable under CPR, r.43.2(1)(a).

Sums paid in settlement of third-party claims.

8–42 [Add to note 39 at end: page 253]
But liability to a third party may constitute recoverable loss notwithstanding that damages have not yet been paid. See *Total Liban SA v. Vitol Energy SA* [2001] Q.B. 643.

[Add to note 40 at end: page 253]
But see the summary of the relevant principles in *P&O Nedlloyd Ltd. v. M&M Militzer & Münch International Holdings AG (The "Marseilles")* [2003] 1 Lloyd's Rep. 503, at para. 128, a case in which the settlement was found to be unreasonable.

4. CONTRACTOR'S BREACH OF CONTRACT

Defective work.

8–47 [Add to note 63 at end: page 256]
See also *Farley v. Skinner (No.2)* [2002] 2 A.C. 732.

[Add to note 65 at end: page 256]
Also *Nordic Holdings v. Mott MacDonald* (2001) 77 Con. L.R. 88 and compare *Southampton Container Terminals Ltd. v. Schiffahrtsgesellschaft "Hansa Australia" (The "Maersk Colombo")* [2001] 2 Lloyd's Rep. 275, CA.

[Add to note 66 at end: page 257]   **8–47A**
Following some doubts, the Court of Appeal in *Burdis v. Livsey* [2003] Q.B. 36 concluded that *Jones v. Stroud* was still good law.

[Add to note 72 after the reference to *Parry v. Cleaver*: page 257]
Arab Bank plc v. John D Wood Commercial Ltd [2000] 1 W.L.R. 857

[Add to note 78 after the reference to *Bigg v. Howard Son & Gooch*: page   **8–48**
258]
Rushmer v. Countrywide Surveyors [2000] P.N.L.R. 529.

[Add to note 80 at end: page 258]
See also *Voaden v. Champion (The "Baltic Surveyor")* [2002] 1 Lloyd's Rep. 623 at paras 85–89 setting out a test of reasonableness.

Inconvenience, discomfort and distress.
[Add to note 2 at end: page 260]   **8–54**
Hoadley v. Edwards [2001] P.N.L.R. 41 (£5,000 where property occupied during remedial works).

[Add to note 4 at end: page 261]
Johnson v. Gore Wood [2002] 2 A.C. 1; *Farley v. Skinner* [2002] 2 A.C. 732. A solicitor's retainer is not such a contract *Channon v. Lindley Johnstone* [2002] P.N.L.R. 884, CA, but an architect's contract to design may be (see note 6).

[Add to text after note 6: page 261]
This decision was overruled in *Farley v. Skinner*[6A] as inconsistent with *Ruxley*.

[6A] [2002] 1 A.C. 1

5. EMPLOYER'S BREACH OF CONTRACT

"Hudson formula"
[Add to note 42 at end: page 268]   **8–69**
For a case in which damages were awarded on the basis of this formula, see *Beechwood Development Company v. Stuart Mitchell* [2001] C.I.L.L. 1727.

Interest for non-payment of money.

8–72 [Add to note 48 at end: page 269]

A series of statutory instruments from November 1998 onwards applied the Act to specified types of commercial contract. S.I. 2002 No.1673 brought the Act into force for all remaining commercial contracts as from August 7, 2002. The Late Payment of Commercial Debts Regulations 2002 also provides for a small additional fixed sum to be paid on qualifying debts.

Simple or compound interest?

8–78 [Add to note 78 at end: page 273]

The Court of Appeal in *Clef Aquitaine SARL v. Laporte Ltd* [2001] Q.B. 488, at 506, was unsure as to whether there was jurisdiction to award compound interest where there was no fiduciary duty but the defendant had acted fraudulently.

CHAPTER 9

TIME FOR COMPLETION AND LIQUIDATED DAMAGES

B. Liquidated Damages

2. DEFENCES TO CLAIM FOR LIQUIDATED DAMAGES

(a) Agreed sum is penalty

Lord Dunedin's propositions.
[Add to note 65 at end: page 282]   **9–14**
See also *Jeancharm Limited v. Barnet Football Club Ltd* [2003] C.I.L.L. 1987, CA, where it was held that an interest rate of 260% per annum was penal.

(g) Extension of time

Condition precendent.
[Add to note 47 at end: page 292]   **9–36A**
In *City Inn Ltd. v. Shepherd Construction Ltd* [2003] C.I.L.L. 2009, the Inner House of the Court of Session held that where the relevant clause required the contractor to give notice, as a condition precedent to an entitlement to an extension of time, the failure to do so did not amount to a breach of contract on the part of the contractor and thus the relevant clause was not a penalty. Although the point set out in the text was not expressly argued it would seem that such an argument would have been rejected on the basis that the entitlement to recover liquidated damages flows not from the

employer's default but the failure of the contractor to operate the contractual machinery.

DEFAULT OF THE PARTIES—VARIOUS MATTERS

1. FORFEITURE CLAUSES

(b) The mode of forfeiture

Compliance with the contract.
[Add to note 14, at end: page 297]   **10–03**
Ellis Tylin Ltd. v. Co-operative Retail Services Ltd [1999] B.L.R. 205.

[Amend note 19: page 297]
Correct typographical error in the reference to the Agricultural Holdings Act 1986.

Ascertainment of the event.
[Add to note 23, at end: page 298]   **10–04**
For a discussion of the Australian approach to "termination for convenience" clauses and whether such clauses are subject to an implied duty of good faith, see Lincoln and Aistrope "Current Issues in the Termination of Construction Contracts" [2002] I.C.L.R. 488.

[Add to text at end: page 298]
Where a contract entitled the employer to terminate the contractor's employment for "breach of any of its obligations under the Contract", it was held that such a clause could only be relied upon where the breach was repudiatory in character or there were an accumulation of breaches that could properly be described as repudiatory.[25A]

[25A] *Rice v. Great Yarmouth Borough Council* [2003] T.C.L.R. 1, CA.

(d) Effect of forfeiture

Employer's claim for damages.
10–11 [Add to note 48 at end, page 301]
See also *Rice v. Great Yarmouth Borough Council* [2003] T.C.L.R. 1, CA.

2. MATERIALS AND PLANT

(a) Ownership of materials and plant

Retention of title clauses.
10–16 [Amend note 67: page 303]
Delete from "Section 395 of the Companies Act 1985 . . ." to end and substitute:

"Section 395 of the Companies Act 1985 would be amended if ss.93 to 107 of the Companies Act 1989 were brought into force. It is not thought that this is likely to happen."

5. GUARANTEES AND BONDS

(a) Guarantees

10–30 [Amend note 20: page 309]
Update the reference to Andrews and Millett, *The Law of Guarantees*, to 3rd ed.

Conduct to prejudice of surety (laches).
10–38 [Add to the text at the end of the first paragraph: page 312]
However where a creditor failed to obtain the proper value of a security,

this did not discharge the surety's liability entirely but reduced *pro tanto* the amount for which the surety was liable.[52A]

[52A] *Skipton Building Society v. Stott* [2000] W.L.R. 103, CA.

(b) Bonds

[Amend note 62: page 313]   **10–41**
Delete the existing note and substitute: See *Halsbury* (4th ed. re-issue), Vol. 13, para. 88.

[Add note 63A after the sentence in the text: "Enforcing the bondsman's liability is colloquially referred to as 'calling the bond'.": page 314]

[63A] "Calling the bond" crystallises the bondsman's liability, so that subsequent events that would render the bond null and void do not affect his liability. See *Alstom Combined Cycles Ltd. v. Henry Boot plc* [2001] All E.R. (D) 12 (May); *OTV Birwelco Ltd. v. Technical and General Guarantee Co. Ltd.* (2002) 84 Con. L.R. 117. It is not a condition precedent of a call on the bond that the beneficiary must first have sued the defaulting party. See *Laing and Morrison Knudson v. Aegon* (1997) 86 B.L.R. 70 and *OTV Birwelco v. Technical and General Guarantee Co. Ltd.*, (see above), at para. 115.

Conditional bonds.
[Add note 66A at the end of the first sentence of the text: page 314]   **10–42**

[66A] To determine whether a bond is conditional or "on demand" it may be necessary to examine the underlying contracts as well as the wording of the bond: *Dragages et Travaux Public (Hong Kong) Ltd. v. Citystate Insurance Ltd.* (2001) Const. L.J. 523, Hong Kong CA.

[Add to note 67 at end, page 314]
OTV Birwelco Ltd. v. Technical and General Guarantee Co. Ltd (2002) 84 Con. L.R. 117.

"On-demand bonds".
[Add to note 75 at end: page 316]   **10–44**
It has been held that for a bond to be construed as "on demand" there should be clear and unambiguous words to this effect: *Dragages et Travaux Public (Hong Kong) Ltd v. Citystate Insurance Ltd* (2001) Const. L.J. 523, Hong Kong CA.

Release by employer.
[Add to text after the penultimate sentence: page 317]   **10–47**
Where a bond provided for the release of the guarantor upon the issue of a Defects Correction Certificate issued in accordance with the terms of the

underlying contract, that release operated prospectively only and did not release the guarantor in respect of liabilities which had crystallised prior to that date. [84A]

[84A] *Alstom Combined Cycles Ltd. v. Henry Boot plc* [2001] All E.R. (D) 12 (May).

6. LIABILITY TO THIRD PARTIES

10–48 [Amend note 87: page 317]
The textbooks referred to are now: *Winfield and Jolowicz* (16th ed.); *Clerk and Lindsell* (18th ed.); *Gale on Easements* (17th ed.).

(b) Nuisance from building operations

Right of support and easements.
10–55 [Amend notes 21 and 22: page 321]
See *Gale on Easements* (17th ed.).

[Add to note 26 at end: page 322]
See also *Rees v. Skerrett* [2001] 1 W.L.R. 1541, CA.

CHAPTER 11

VARIOUS EQUITABLE DOCTRINES AND REMEDIES

1. ESTOPPEL

Estoppel by representation.

[Add to note 4, after reference to *Avon v. Howlett*: page 327]   **11–02**
For a consideration of this latter case see: *National Westminster Bank plc v. Somer International (UK) Ltd* [2001] EWCA Civ 970; [2002] Q.B. 1286. In that case a bank claimed re-payment of sums transferred by mistake. It was held that equity would limit a defence based on estoppel to the extent of the detriment suffered.

2. WAIVER

[Amend note 16 at end: page 329]   **11–05**
[Chitty] para. 23–039

[Insert new paragraph 11–07A: page 329]
By virtue of section 108 of the Housing Grants, Construction and **11–07A** Regeneration Act 1996, parties to a construction contract have a statutory right to refer disputes arising under that contract to adjudication.[21A] That right is not waived by the issue of court proceedings in respect of the same dispute.[21B] A party's right to object to an adjudicator's jurisdiction may be waived by making a request that he corrects his decision, or by making a payment in respect of that decision.[21C]

[21A] See para. 16–100.
[21B] *Herschel Engineering Ltd. v. Breen Property Ltd.* [2000] B.L.R. 272
[21C] *Shimizu Europe Ltd. v. Automajor Ltd.* [2002] B.L.R. 113

5. SPECIFIC PERFORMANCE

Building agreement.
[Add to note 66 at end: page 335]   **11–20**

An order for specific performance may also be made in respect of a tenant's repairing covenants where the landlord has no right to repair, *Rainbow Estates Ltd. v. Tokenhold Ltd.* [1999] Ch. 64.

6. INJUNCTION

11–22 [Add to note 71 at end: page 336]
, although disapproved in *Jaggard v. Sawyer* [1995] 1 W.L.R. 269, CA.

Injunction to enforce disputed forfeiture.
11–24 [Add to note 84 at end: page 337]
In the case of a mandatory injunction different principles apply. See *Nottingham Building Society v. Eurodynamics Systems* [1993] F.S.R. 468 approved in *Zockoll Group Ltd. v. Mercury Communications Ltd (No.1)* [1998] F.S.R. 354, CA.

CHAPTER 12

ASSIGNMENTS, SUBSTITUTED CONTRACTS AND SUB-CONTRACTS

1. ASSIGNMENTS

(a) Assignment by contractor of burden

Novation.

[Add new paragraph at end: page 340]   **12–03**

A contractor who takes a novation from the employer of a consultant's appointment may not be entitled to damages resulting from breaches by the consultant of obligations already performed for the employer.[5a]

[5A] *Blyth & Blyth Ltd v. Carillion Construction Ltd* (2001) 79 Con. L.R. 142.

(b) Assignment by contractor of benefit

[Add to note 26 at end: page 342]   **12–07**

Raiffeisen Zentralbank Österreich AG v. Five Star General Trading LLC [2001] EWCA Civ 68; [2001] Q.B. 825

Consideration.

12–13 [Add to note 61 at end: page 345]
See also *Raiffeisen Zentralbank Österreich AG v. Five Star General Trading LLC* [2001] EWCA Civ 68; [2001] Q.B. 825

Subject to equities.

12–14 [Add to note 65 at end: page 346]
In *Business Computers Ltd v. Anglo-African Leasing Ltd.* [1977] 1 W.L.R. 578 it was said that ". . . a debt which accrues due before notice of an assignment is received, whether or not it is payable before that date, or a debt which arises out of the same contract as that which gives rise to the assigned debt, or is closely connected with that contract, may be set off against the assignee. A debt with is neither accrued not connected may not be set off even though it arises from a contract made before the assignment."

(d) Assignment by employer of burden

Maintenance, champerty and assignment of causes of action.

12–21 [Add to note 88 at end: page 349]
For public policy considerations see *R.(Factortame Ltd) v. Secretary of State for Transport, Local Government and the Regions (No. 8)* [2002] EWCA Civ 932; [2003] Q.B. 381.

[Add to note 91 at end: page 349]
Bevan Ashford v. Geoff Yeandle (Contractors) Ltd [1999] Ch. 239.

Assignment of warranties.

12–23A [Amend reference at note 7: page 351]
Alfred McAlpine Construction Ltd v. Panatown Ltd is now reported at [2001] 1 A.C. 518.

5. RELATIONSHIP BETWEEN SUB-CONTRACTOR AND MAIN CONTRACTOR

Set-off.

12–62 [Replace second sentence in note 26 with the following: page 370]
Where no valid s. 111 notice has been served neither a right of set-off (*Northern Developments (Cumbria) Ltd v. J & J Nichol* (unreported, TCC 24/1/00)) nor of abatement (*Whiteways Contractors (Sussex) Ltd v. Impresa Castelli Construction UK Ltd* (2001) 75 Con. L.R. 92) may be relied upon to withhold payment. See para. 15–15H for a fuller analysis.

[Add to note 30 at end: page 370]
However, where the Housing Grants, Construction and Regeneration Act 1996 applies, a valid notice under s. 111 may be required in order to

withhold payment on the grounds of a right of set-off or abatement. See n. 26 above and para. 15–15H.

CHAPTER 13

ARCHITECTS, ENGINEERS AND SURVEYORS

2. MEANING AND USE OF THE TERM "ARCHITECT"

13–02 [Add to note 3: page 374]
The obligation of the architect may not generally be to "supervise": see, for instance, the obligation to visit the Works in condition 2.8 of the Standard Form of Agreement at para. C-1 l of the main work.

3. REGISTRATION

Use of title "architect".
13–03 [Add to note 63: page 380]
Munkenbeck and Marshall v. Kensington Hotel (1999) 15 Const. L.J. 231.

4. THE POSITION OF THE ARCHITECT

(c) Excess of authority by architect

Position of the employer.
13–22 [Amend note 74: page 381]

The reference should now be to *Bowstead and Reynolds on Agency* (17th ed., Sweet & Maxwell, 2001), p.307.

[Add to note 74: page 381]
Credit Lyonnais Bank Nederland NV v. Export Credits Guarantee Department [2000] 1 A.C. 486, HL.

[Amend note 82: page 382]
The reference should now be to *Bowstead and Reynolds on Agency* (17th ed.) p.67.

(d) Architect's personal liability on contracts

[Amend note 92: page 383]   13–26
The reference should now be to *Bowstead and Reynolds on Agency* (17th ed.), Art. 100.

[Amend note 93: page 383]
The reference should now be to *Bowstead and Reynolds on Agency* (17th ed.), Arts 78 and 100.

[Amend note 94: page 384]
The reference should now be to *Bowstead and Reynolds on Agency* (17th ed.), Art. 101.

(e) Fraudulent misrepresentation

[Add to note 98: page 384]   13–27
Credit Lyonnais Bank Nederland NV v. Export Credits Guarantee Department [2000] 1 A.C. 486, HL

(g) Architects' duties to the employer

[Amend note 24: page 387]   13–33
The reference should now be to *Bowstead and Reynolds on Agency* (17th ed.).

Expert evidence.
[Add to note 51: page 390]   13–39
After the reference to *University of Glasgow v. Whitfield* add *Nordic Holdings Ltd v. Mott MacDonald Ltd* (2001) 77 Con. L.R. 88 at 121.

[Amend note 52: page 390]
Sansom v. Metcalfe is now reported at [1998] P.N.L.R. 542.

(h) Architects' duties in detail

Design.

13–55 [Add to note 6: page 397]

The duty to review the design only arises when something occurs to put the architect on notice that, as a reasonably competent architect, he ought to review the design: *New Islington and Hackney Housing Association Ltd v. Pollard Thomas and Edwards Ltd* [2001] B.L.R. 74 at 80.

[Add to note 8: page 397]

Whether an architect is under a contractual duty to review his design after practical completion depends on the architect's conditions of engagement read with the building contract: *New Islington and Hackney Housing Association Ltd v. Pollard Thomas and Edwards Ltd* [2001] B.L.R. 74 at 80.

Supervision.

13–62 [Add to first sentence of note 32: page 400]

and see the explanation of *Corfield v. Grant* in *Consarc Design Ltd v. Hutch Investments Ltd* (2002) 84 Con. L.R. 36 at 59 which adopts with approval paras 8–236 to 8–249 of *Jackson & Powell on Professional Negligence* (5th ed., Sweet & Maxwell, 2002). In particular, in relation to supervision, an architect's duty is to exercise reasonable skill and care in seeking to achieve a particular result; he does not guarantee that a particular result will be achieved or that his inspection will reveal or prevent all defective work.

(k) Remuneration

Amount of remuneration.

13–89 [Add to note 27: page 412]

For a recent application *of Way v. Latilla*, see *Vedatech Corporation v. Crystal Decisions (UK) Ltd* [2002] EWHC 818 (Ch).

THE EUROPEAN COMMUNITY

2. PROCUREMENT

Procurement legislation.

[Add to note 39: page 432]   **14–09**

See also Case C-411/00 *Felix Swoboda GmbH v. Osterreichische Nationalbank*, unreported, November 14, 2002.

[Amend note 41: page 432]

Case C-380/98 *R. v. H.M. Treasury Ex p. The University of Cambridge* is now reported at [2000] E.C.R. I-8035.

[Add to note 341: page 432]

See also Case C-399/98 *Ordine degli Architetti delle Province di Milano e Lodi* [2000] E.C.R. I-5409 ("public works contract"); Case C-237/99 *Commission v. France (OPAC)* [2001] E.C.R. I-939 (meaning of "management supervision" by state); Case C-470/99 *Universale-Bau v. EBS* [2002] ECR I-11617 (definition of "contracting authority"); joined cases C-223 & 260/99, *Agora* [2001] E.C.R. I-3605 (criterion of specific establishment of an entity to meet needs in general interest not having a commercial or industrial character); Case C-373/00 *Adolf Truly GmbH v. Bestattung Wien GmbH* (February 27, 2003) (concept of "contracting authority"); Case C-18/01 *Arkkitehtuuritoimisto Riita Korhonen Oy v. Vorkauden Taitotalo Oy* (May 22, 2003) ("contracting authority"); Arrowsmith "Public private partnerships and the European Procurement rules: EU policies in conflict" 37 C.M.L.R. 709.

[Replace note 43: page 432]
[2000] E.C.R. I-8377.

[Amend note 47: page 433]
Case C-324/98 *Telaustria Verlags GmbH & Telefonadress GmbH v. Post & Telekom Austria A.G.* is now reported at [2000] E.C.R. I-10745.

[Add to note 47: page 433]
See also Case C-59/00 *Bent Mousten Vestergaard v. Spøttrup Boligselskab* [2001] E.C.R. I-9505 (although certain contracts are excluded from the scope of the Community directives in the field of public procurement, the contracting authorities which conclude them are nevertheless bound to comply with the fundamental rules of the Treaty).

14-10 [Add to note 52: page 433]
See also Case C-16/98 *Commission v. France* [2000] E.C.R. I-8315.

Contracting authorities have certain choices of procedure.
14-13 [Add to note 59: page 435]
See also the Commission's Interpretative Communication on the Community law applicable to public procurement and the possibilities for integrating social considerations into public procurement, COM (2001) 566.

[Add to note 60: page 435]
See also Case C-94/99 *ARGE* [2000] E.C.R. I-11037

[Add to note 61: page 435]
In *Luck v. London Borough of Tower Hamlets* [2003] EWCA Civ 52, the Court of Appeal said (*obiter*) that there *may* be a duty to disclose the minimum financial and technical requirements applicable. However, the Court of Appeal was not referred to Case C-470/99 *Universale-Bau v. EBS* [2002] E.C.R. I-11617 in which the ECJ held that they *must* be disclosed.

14-14 [Add to note 71: page 436]
See Joined Cases C-20/01 and C-28/01 *Commission v. Germany*, unreported April 10, 2003, for the limits on the ability to derogate from the rules in the context of public service contracts.

[Add to note 72: page 436]
See also Joined Cases C-285 & 286/99 *Impresa Lombardini SpA v. ANAS* [2001] E.C.R. I-9233 (mathematical criteria may be used to identify and abnormally low tender provided an opportunity is given to the tenderer to clarify the tender); Case C-94/99 *ARGE* [2000] E.C.R. I-11037 (relevance of existence of state subsidy where tender); and on the relationship between public procurement and state aids see Bartosch "The Relationship between Public Procurement and State Aid Surveillance — The Toughest Standard Applies?" (39 C.M.L.R. 551).

[Substitute the last three sentences of the text with the following: page 437]
In Case C-225/98 *Commission v. France* [2000] E.C.R. I-7445 the ECJ held that a criterion linked to a campaign against unemployment is allowed by the Treaty provided that it is consistent with all the fundamental principles of Community law, in particular the principle of non-discrimination.

[Substitute note 78 with the following: page 437]
See also Case C-19/00 *SIAC Construction Ltd v. The County Council of the County of Mayo* [2001] E.C.R. I-7725; Case C-513/99 *Concordia Bus Finland Oy AB v. Helsingin Kaupunki and HKL-Bussilükenne* [2002] E.C.R. I-7213 and noted in [2003] C.M.L.R. 179 (environmental considerations as award criteria).

[Add to note 82A: page 438]   14–15
See Case C-92/00 *Hospital Ingenieure Krankenhaustechnik Planungs-GmbH (HI) v. Stadt Wien* [2002] E.C.R. I-5553 (decision to abandon award procedure must be open to effective review).

[Add to note 72: page 436]
See Case T-5/99 *Andriotis v. Commission of the European Communities* [2000] E.C.R. II-235 (disappointed tenderer has no standing to force publication in Official Journal of information already obtained by other means).

Remedies.
[Add to note 93: page 439]   14–18
The case proceeded in the High Court ([2002] EWHC 717) and in the Court of Appeal as *Luck v. London Borough of Tower Hamlets* [2003] EWCA Civ 52.

[Add to note 96: page 440]
See also Case C-327/00 *Santex v. Unita Socio Sanitaria Locale n.42 di Pavia*, unreported, Februry 27, 2003 (national limitation periods not objectionable provided they are reasonable and do not make remedies excessively difficult to obtain).

[Add to note 97: page 440]
See also the Court of Appeal in *Jobsin.co.uk plc v. Dept of Health* [2001] Eu.L.R. 685 (ignorance of legal rights and commercial considerations *not* good reasons to extend time).

[Add new note 98A at end of text: page 440]
See now Case C-424/01 *CS Communications & Systems Austria GmbH v. Allgemeine Unfallversicherungsanstalt*, unreported, April 9, 2003—duty or discretion of the body responsible for review procedures to take account of the prospects of success of the substantive claim; also in the English High Court, *Severn Trent Water plc v. Welsh Water Ltd* [2001] Eu.L.R. 136 (factors relevant to the grant and form of relief).

Implied contract

14–19 [Add new note 10A at end of text: page 441]

See however the discussion of the common law position after *Harmon* by Craig, "Developments in the Law of Tenders: Radical or Evolutionary Development?" (2003) 19 Const. L.J. 237.

Reform of community procurement law

14–21 [Add to note 15: page 442]

Agreement on a Commission Position was reached between the Council and Commission on May 21, 2002. The process now awaits the decision of the European Parliament on its second reading under the co-decision procedure. See Williams *Update on the European Commission's Proposal to Amend the Public Sector Procurement Directives: Adoption of a Common Position* (2003) 12 P.P.L.R. N.A. 1. See also (2000) 9 P.P.L.R. N.A. 125 for an outline of the proposals.

3. RESTRICTIVE AGREEMENTS AND COMPETITION

E.C. competition law.

14–25 [Add new note 26A at the end of the first sentence: page 444]

On the meaning of "undertaking" see *Bettercare v. Director General of Fair Trading*, August 1, 2002, The Competition Commission Appeal Tribunal, (discussed in (2003) 12 P.P.L.R. N.A. 71) and Case T-19/99 *Fenin v. Commission*, unreported, April 3, 2003. Both cases are discussed in Skilbeck "Just when is a Public Body an "Undertaking"? Fenin and Bettercare compared" (2003) 12 P.P.L.R. N.A. 75. See also Case C-309/99 *Wouters, Savelbergh, Price Waterhouse Belastingadviseurs BV v. Algemene Raad van de Nederlandse Orde van Advocaten* [2002] E.C.R. I-1577 (association of legal and the "liberal" professions as "undertakings") and Case C-218/00 *Cisal di Battistello Venanzio & C. Sas. v.* Inail [2002] E.C.R. I-691 (whether public non-profit-making insurance body an "undertaking").

[Add to note 27: page 444]

See also Case T-41/96 *Bayer AG v. EC Commission* [2000] E.C.R. II-3383

14–26 [Add new note 32A at end of first paragraph: page 445]

Commission Regulation (EC) 2790/1999 of December 22, 1999 on the application of Art. 81(3) of the Treaty to categories of vertical agreements and concerted practices ([1999] O.J. L336/21) states that, under certain conditions, Art. 81(1) does not apply to agreements or concerted practices entered into between two or more undertakings each of which operates, for the purposes of the agreement, at a different level of the production or distribution chain, and relating to the conditions under which the parties may purchase, sell or resell certain goods or services. This Regulation was unsuccessfully challenged in Case C-341/00P *Conseil national des professions de l'automobile v.* Commission [2000] E.C.R. I-5236.

[Add to note 27: page 444]
For further examples see Case C-214/99 *Neste Markkinointi Oy v. Yötuuli Ky* [2000] E.C.R. I-11121; Case T-62/98 *Volkswagen AG v. EC Commission* [2000] E.C.R. II-2707 (appealed in Case-338/00P, Opinion of A.-G. Ruiz-Jarabo Colomer, October 17, 2002); Case C-475/99 *Ambulanz Glöckner v. Landkreis Südwestpfalz* [2001] E.C.R. I-8089.

[Amend note 37–38: page 445]   **14–27**
Appeal in *Campagnie Maritime Belge Transport v. Commission* is now reported as C-395/96 & 396/96 at [2000] E.C.R. I-1365

[Add to note 37–38: page 445]
For further cases considering abuse of a dominant position, see Case C-428/98 *Deutsche Post AG v. International Express Carriers Conference (IECC)* [2000] E.C.R. I-3061 (Order); [2001] 4 C.M.L.R. 117; Case T-513/93 *Consiglio Nazionale degli Spedizionieri Doganali v. EC Commission* [2000] E.C.R. II-1807; [2000] 5 C.M.L.R. 614; Case T-128/98 *Aéroports de Paris v. EC Commission* [2000] E.C.R. II-3929; [2001] 4 C.M.L.R. 1376 (unsuccessfully appealed in Case C-82/01P).

[Add to note 41: page 446]
In Case C-344/98 *Masterfoods Ltd v. HB Ice Cream Ltd; HB Ice Cream Ltd v. Masterfoods Ltd* [2000] E.C.R. I-11369 the ECJ held that where a national court is ruling on an agreement or practice, the compatibility of which with Arts 85(1) and 86 of the EC Treaty (now Arts 81(1) and 82) is already the subject of a Commission decision, it cannot take a decision running counter to that of the Commission, even if the latter's decision conflicts with a decision given by a national court of first instance. For a series of cases in which the Commission found breaches of Art. 81(1) and imposed fines but faced extensive challenges to its Decisions see Joined Cases T-25/95 (and others) *Cimenteries CBR SA v. EC Commission* [2000] E.C.R. II-491 (currently under appeal in a number of cases before the ECJ). See also Joined Cases T-125/97 and T-127/97 *Coca-Cola Company v. EC Commission* [2000] E.C.R. II-1733; [2000] 5 C.M.L.R. 467 (mere finding in the contested decision that a company holds a dominant position has no binding legal effects so that the applicants' challenge to its merits is not admissible)

Remedies for violation of E.C. competition law.
14-28 [Amend Note 43: page 446]
Crehan has now been decided as Case C-453/99 *Courage Ltd v. Bernhard Crehan* [2001] E.C.R. I-6297; [2001] 5 C.M.L.R. 1058.

14-29 [Add to note 46: page 447]
For unsuccessful applications for injunctions in the English courts see (under Art. 82) *Sockel GmbH v. The Body Shop International plc* [2000] Eu.L.R. 276; (under the Competition Act 1998) *Getmapping plc v. Ordnance Survey* [2002] Eu.L.R. 464 and *Suretrack Rail Services Limited v. Infraco JNP Ltd* [2002] Eu.L.R. 659.

U.K. Competition Act 1998

14-30 [Add note at end: page 448]
Section 2 of the Act establishes a general prohibition on "agreements between undertakings, decisions by associations of undertakings or concerted practices which (a) may affect trade within the United Kingdom, and (b) have as their object or effect the prevention, restriction or distortion of competition within the United Kingdom". However, this general prohibition is subject to exceptions including, importantly, the exclusion from it of "vertical agreements" by virtue of The Competition Act 1998 (Land and Vertical Agreements Exclusion) Order 2000 (S.I. 2000 No. 310).

[Add new text: page 448]

14-30A **The Enterprise Act 2000.** Section 188 creates a new offence called the Cartel Offence. Section 188(1) imposes criminal liability if an individual dishonestly agrees with one or more other persons to make or implement, or to cause to be made or implemented, arrangements of a defined type relating to at least two undertakings. Sections 188 (2) and (3) define those arrangements as including ones which, if operating as the parties to the agreement intend, would fix a price for the supply by A in the United Kingdom (otherwise than to B) of a product or service, limit or prevent supply or production by A in the United Kingdom of a product or service, divide between A and B the supply in the United Kingdom of a product or service to a customer or customers for the supply in the United Kingdom of a product or serivce be bid-rigging arrangements.

5. HARMONISATION OF CIVIL LIABILITY

14-34 [Add to note 58: page 449]
see Editorial Comments, "On the way to a European Contract Code?" [2002] 39 C.M.L.R. 219.

CHAPTER 15

VARIOUS LEGISLATION

1. DEFECTIVE PREMISES ACT 1972

The duty to build dwellings properly.
[Add to note 16 at end: page 452]   **15–03A**
Lee v. Leeds C.C. [2002] 1 W.L.R. 1488, CA; *Dunn v. Bradford Metropolitan D.C.* [2002] 3 E.G.L.R. 104, CA.

Limitation of actions.
[Add to text after note 24: page 454]   **15–07**
Thus a fresh cause of action will accrue where further work is carried out which fails to rectify a defect in the original work even though that further work is itself properly executed.[24A]

[24A] *Alderson v. Beetham Organisation Ltd* [2003] B.L.R. 217, CA.

[Add to text after note 25: page 454]
Section 14A of the Limitation Act 1980 does not apply to claims under the DPA.[25A]

[25A] *Samuel Payne v. John Setchell Ltd* [2002] B.L.R. 489.

2. CONTROL OF POLLUTION ACT 1974 AND ENVIRONMENTAL PROTECTION ACT 1990

The Environmental Protection Act 1990.

15–12 [Add to note 46 at end: page 456]
See also regulations S.I. 1998 No. 767 and S.I. 2000 No. 1973.

Statutory nuisances.

[Add to note 53 at end: page 457]
Section 79(1)(a) of the 1990 Act is directed at the presence in premises of some feature in itself prejudicial to health as a source of possible infection, disease or illness and does not extend to the layout of the premises, unavoidable use within the layout, or the facilities that ought to be installed—*Birmingham City Council v. Oakley* [2001] 1 A.C. 617, HL. See also *Griffiths v. Pembrokeshire County Council, The Times* April 19, 2000, DC—the smell of smoke, without there being any visible particles, was sufficient to constitute a smoke nuisance under s.79(1)(b) of the Environmental Protection Act 1990.

15–15 [Amend note 56: page 457]
Delete "1985, 1988,". These regulations were revoked; see Noise Emission in the Environment by Equipment for Use Outdoors Regulations 2001, (S.I. 2001 No. 1701).

3. HOUSING GRANTS, CONSTRUCTION AND REGENERATION ACT 1996, PART II

Application of Part II.

15–15C [Add to note 73 at end: page 459]
In *Yarm Road v. Costain Ltd* (unreported) February 27, 2001 (H.H. Judge Havery Q.C.) it was held that a contract entered into before May 1, 1998 but novated after that date was a construction contract within the meaning of s.104(6)(a). However a Deed of Variation, which altered the fees to be paid for managing the undertaking of a building development, entered into after the Act came into force was not a construction contract—*Earls Terrace Properties Limited v. Waterloo Investments Limited* [2002] C.I.L.L. 1890.

[Add new text after the fifth sentence: page 459]
Contract administration falls within the Act,[75A] however providing evidence or assisting with an arbitration does not.[75B]

[75A] *Gillies Ramsay Diamond v. PJE Enterprises Ltd* [2003] B.L.R. 48.
[75B] *Fence Gate Ltd v. James R Knowles Ltd* (2001) 84 Con. L.R. 206.

[Add new text after reference to note 81: page 459]
Subsections 105(1)(a), (b) and (c) refer to various operations but with the added description "forming, or to form, part of the land" (and which are clearly not required in subsections (d), (e) and (f)) with the result that certain construction operations must involve structures forming, or to form, part of the land. Therefore shop fitting is excluded [81A] as are structures to be founded in the sea bed below low water mark.[81B] However operations which "form an integral part of, or are preparatory to, or are for rendering complete construction operations" are themselves construction operations.[81C]

[81A] At least where the fittings are only attached to land for purposes of stability: *Gibson Lea Retail Interiors Ltd v. Makro Self Service Ltd* [2001] B.L.R. 407
[81B] *Stavely Industries PLC v. Odebrecht Oil & Gas Services Ltd,* (unreported) February 27, 2001 (H.H. Judge Havery Q.C.).
[81C] Section 105(1)(e). Thus a contract between a contractor and an owner of a crane for the hire of a mobile crane plus driver was held to be a contract for construction operations which formed an integral part of, or were preparatory to, or were for rendering complete, construction operations within s.105(1)(a)—*Baldwins Industrial Services Plc v. Barr Ltd* [2003] B.L.R. 176.

[Add to note 84B at end: page 460]
The site as a whole must be considered (*i.e.* not necessarily the "site" as might be defined by the construction contract) as must the primary purpose of the whole site in order to determine the primary activity—*ABB Zantingh v. Zedal Building Services* [2001] B.L.R. 66.

[Add new text after reference to note 87: page 460]
Where a contract relates to construction operations and other matters, the Act applies to that contract "only so far as it relates to construction operations", see section 104(5) of the Act. It remains to be seen how this difficult provision is applied in practice, in particular in relation to rights and obligations which may not be readily divisible. It is to be noted that whilst section 105(1) defines the operations that are included by a description of the construction operation, subsections 105(2)(a), (b) and (c) define the exclusion from construction operations in terms of the object of the construction operation. Thus drilling or extraction of oil or natural gas are excluded operations. This can give rise to difficulty where the main

contractor's work may fall within one of the exclusions in subsection 105(2) whereas a sub-contractor, being only concerned with a small part of the overall works, may be carrying out a construction operation within section 105(1).[87A]

[87A] Compare the approach in *Palmers Ltd v. ABB Power Construction Ltd* (1999) 68 Con. L.R. 52, with the approach in *ABB Power Construction Ltd v. Norwest Holst Engineering* (2001) T.C.L.R. 831. In the first case, H.H. Judge Thornton Q.C. held that it was possible for a contractor's operations to fall outside the Act but for his sub-contractor's operations to fall within the Act. In the second, H.H. Judge Lloyd Q.C. held that the object of s. 105(2)(a)-(d) is that "all the construction operations necessary to achieve the aims or purposes of the owner or of the principal contractors (as described therein) would be exempt", including sub-contractor's.

Agreement in writing.

15–15D [Amend the text following reference to note 94: page 460]

Delete the sentences: "It is not clear whether an agreement partly in writing and partly made orally is covered by the Act. It is submitted it is, since there no requirement that the whole of the agreement is set out in writing." Substitute: Further there is an agreement in writing where "the agreement is evidenced in writing."[94A] In *RJT Consulting Engineers Ltd v. DM Engineering (Northern Ireland)*[94B] the majority of the Court of Appeal (Ward and Robert Walker L.JJ.) emphasised that the whole of the contract had to be evidenced in writing, not merely part of it. It was not sufficient to confer jurisdiction that there was evidence in writing going merely to the existence or substance of an agreement, the parties to it and the nature of the work and price. Thus an oral variation of material terms of a contract also had to be evidenced in writing to satisfy the definition.[94C]

[94A] s.107(2)(c).
[94B] [2002] 1 W.L.R. 2344, CA.
[94C] *Carillion Construction Ltd v. Devonport Royal Dockyard* [2003] B.L.R. 79. *Cf. Total M&E Services Ltd. v. Building Technologies Ltd* (2002) 87 Con. L.R. 154, where H.H. Judge Wilcox decided, relying upon s.107(3) of the Act, that oral variations (to increase workscope) of a contract without a variations clause fell within the Act. *Total M&E* was decided before both the above-referred to cases and it is suggested should be approached with caution.

Periodic payments and determining when payment is due.

15–15F [Add to note 99 at end: page 462]

A mere failure to give the notice required by s. 110(2) does not prevent a dispute arising in adjudication about the sum claimed—see *SL Timber v. Carillion* [2001] B.L.R. 516; see also *Maxi Construction Management Ltd* [2001] C.I.L.L. 1784.

15–15G [Add to note 2 at end: page 462]

In *C&B Scene v. Isobars* [2001] C.I.L.L. 1781, the parties had failed to elect between alternative payment provisions contained in the JCT 1998 form. In those circumstances it was held that the contract did not contain payment provisions which complied with the Act and so the whole of the JCT terms fell away and the Scheme applied (reversed by the Court of Appeal on different grounds).

Withholding of moneys.

[Add to note 8 at end: page 462]   **15–15H**
The notice must also be in writing—*Strathmore Building Services Ltd v. Colin Scott Greig* (2001) 17 Const. L.J. 72.

[Add to note 9 at end: page 462]
The notice cannot be served before the application for payment is received—*Strathmore Building Services Ltd v. Colin Scott Greig* (2001) 17 Const. L.J. 72.

[Add to note 10 at end: page 463]
See also Ian Duncan Wallace Q.C., "The HGCRA: A Critical Lacuna" (2002) 18 Const. L.J. 117; Ian Duncan Wallace Q.C., "HGCRA Section 111(2) 'Wrong Answer to Right Question?'" (2003) 19 Const. L.J. 187; and Peter Sheridan and Dominic Helps, "Construction Act Review" (2002) 18 Const. L.J. 224.

[Add to note 12 at end: page 463]
Just such an approach was adopted by the Court of Appeal in *Rupert Morgan Building Services (LLC). v. David Jervis* (unreported, November 13, 2003). The defendants claimed to be able to raise certain defences for non-payment which did not require a withholding notice. Those defences were (i) work not done at all (ii) duplication (iii) claimed extras within contract and (iv) claimed work was correcting defects. The Court of Appeal found, on the terms of the contract, that it was not the actual work done which defined the "sum due" for the purposes of s.111, but simply the amount identified in the interim certificate. The Court of Appeal therefore decided that none of the defences could succeed without a withholding notice, whether those defences were characterised as set-off, claims for breaches reducing the sum due, abatement "and so on". Without a withholding notice, the sum identified in the certificate would have to be paid. Note, however, that the Court of Appeal merely distinguished the decision in *SL Timber Systems*, rather than deciding whether or not on its facts it was correct; that the full valuation and payment terms of the contract at issue are not apparent from the text of the judgments and that it is not clear from the decision whether the said contract was Act-compliant, or whether the Scheme applied. It therefore remains to be seen what is left of the argument identified in the text in cases where the payment terms do not identify the sum payable by reference to the interim certificate, and in certain Scheme cases. However, it seems clear that this decision, and thus the proposition in the text, will apply to the certification and payment provisions in most standard forms.

[Add to text at end of paragraph: page 463]

It seems that a party cannot withhold payment against an adjudicator's award by virtue of cross claims and set offs even if he issues a notice of intention to withhold payment after the award is issued.[13A] If, on a proper construction, the adjudicator's decision is as to a sum which will become due in the future, as opposed to a sum already due, then a withholding notice may be validly served providing the sum awarded has not in the meantime become due.[13B]

[13A] *VHE Construction plc v. RBSTB Trust Co Ltd* [2000] B.L.R. 187; *Solland International Ltd v. Daryan Ltd* (2002) 83 Con. L.R. 109; *Construction Group Centre v. Highland Council* [2002] B.L.R. 476. Further, a contract term which seeks to override the statutory obligation to comply with the adjudicator's award will not be effective: see *Ferson Contractors v. Levolux* [2003] B.L.R. 118, disapproving *Bovis Lend Lease Ltd v. Triangle Development Ltd* [2003] B.L.R. 31 and, it seems, *KNS v. Sindall* 75 Con. L.R. 71. *Cf. David McClean Housing Contractors v. Swansea Housing Association* [2002] B.L.R. 125, where the sum found payable by the adjudicator was incorporated into a certificate against which the employer issued an effective notice of intention to withhold payment. See further Chap. 16, s.11.

[13B] *Shimiza Europe Ltd. v. LBJ Fabrications Ltd.* [2003] B.L.R. 381.

Partial exclusion of "pay-when-paid" clauses.

15–15J [Add to text at end of paragraph: page 464]

A pay when paid clause is not of itself unreasonable for the purposes of Unfair Contract Terms Act 1977[18A]

[18A] *Durabella v. Jarvis* 83 Con. L.R. 145.

4. LIMITATION ACT 1980 AND LATENT DAMAGE ACT 1986

15–16 [Add note 18A at the end of the first sentence: page 464]

The Law Commission has published its Report, *Limitation of Actions* Law Commission No. 270 (2001) which recommends substantial reform to the Limitation Act 1980.

Contract.

15–17 [Add note 29A at the end of the first sentence of the second paragraph: page 465]

See *Tameside Metropolitan B.C. v. Barlows Securities Group Ltd* [2001] B.L.R. 113, CA.

[Add new text after second sentence of the second paragraph: page 465]

In the usual case a cause of action in contract against a designer arises, at latest, on practical completion of the works unless a fresh duty arises to reconsider the design in the light of defects manifesting themselves subsequent to practical completion.[29B]

[29B] *University Court of Glasgow v William Whitfield and John Laing Construction Ltd* (1988) 42 B.L.R. 66; *New Islington & Hackney Housing Association v. Pollard Thomas and Edwards* [2001] B.L.R. 74.

Tort.

[Add to note 31 at end: page 465]   **15–18**
An action for damages for an infringement of the European Communities Act 1972 of rights conferred by Community Law amounted to a breach of statutory duty and could therefore be considered "an action founded on tort" for the purposes of this section of the Limitation Act—*R. v. Secretary of State for Transport Ex p. Factortame Ltd (No.6)* [2001] 1 W.L.R. 942. See also Chap. 14.

[Add to note 34 at end: page 466]
In *Murphy v. Brentwood D.C.* [1991] A.C. 398 the House of Lords "re-interpreted" the decision in *Pirelli* as being one of economic loss rather than physical damage. However the House of Lords did not say it had been wrongly decided. If it was a case of economic loss then, consistent with authority, the cause of action would have accrued on the date when the defective chimney was constructed to the defective design or, consistent with the Australian authority of *Council of the Shire of Sutherland v. Heyman* 157 C.L.R. 424, on the date when the defect was discovered or discoverable. See the discussion in *New Islington and Hackney Housing Association Limited v. Pollard Thomas and Edwards Ltd* [2001] B.L.R. 74.

[Add to text at end of paragraph: page 466]
Progressive damage originating from one act or omission creates a single cause of action arising when more than negligible damage has occurred.[34A]

[34A] See, for example, *Homburg Houtimport BV v. Agrosin Private Ltd, The "Starsin"* [2001] Lloyd's Rep. 437, CA, in particular at para. 105, and see also *Knapp v. Ecclesiastical Insurance Group Plc* [1998] P.N.L.R. 172, CA.

[Add to note 36 after the reference to paragraph 7–13: page 466]   **15–19**
The "complex structure theory" is probably best to be regarded as no longer tenable. See *Samuel Payne v. John Setchell Ltd* [2002] B.L.R. 489.

[Add note 36 at end: page 466]
Whilst these cases are obsolete they are still regularly referred to an analysed in the judgments. See, for example, *Tesco Stores Ltd v. Costain Construction Ltd* (unreported) July 2, 2003 (H.H. Judge Seymour Q.C.).

[Add new note 36A after the word "advice" in the first sentence of the second paragraph: page 466]
The original category of "negligent misstatement or advice" has been widened on high authority, notably Lord Steyn, to include the provision of services (usually professional but often merely specialised) generally. See in particular *MacFarlane v. Tayside Health Authority* [2000] 2 A.C. 59, HL, where Lord Steyn states that the "extended *Hedley Byrne* principle" is "simply the rationalisation adopted by the common law to provide a remedy for the recovery of economic loss for a species of negligently performed services", an idea Lord Steyn first raised in *Williams v. Natural Health Foods Ltd* [1998] 1 W.L.R. 830, HL. Identifying the date of the accrual of a cause of action based on a specific piece of advice or a specific statement is already problematic. Such problems only increase when the complaint concerns "services", and the application of the test provided by *Forster v. Outred & Co.* [1982] 1 W.L.R. 86 at page 94, adopted by the House of Lords in *Nykredit Mortgage Bank plc. v. Edward Erdman Ltd* [1997] 1 W.L.R. 1627, leads to surprising results. For an example of a recent TCC case applying the *Forster* test literally see *Tesco Stores Ltd v. Costain Construction Ltd* (unreported) July 2, 2003 (H.H. Judge Seymour Q.C.) at paras 250–252.

[Add to note 38 at end: page 466]
Proctor v. Gamble v. Carrier Holdings [2003] B.L.R. 255.

[Add to note 39 at end: page 467]
Byrne v. Pain and Foster [1999] 1 W.L.R. 1849.

[Add the following text as a new paragraph after the last paragraph: page 467]
There has been little direct English authority as to when the cause of action in tort accrues where the loss is solely economic, involves no physical damage and does not result from negligent misstatement or advice. Thus in *Tozer Kemsley and Millbourn (Holdings) Ltd v J Jarvis & Sons Ltd*, it was held that the cause of action for the negligent design of a defective heating and air conditioning system arose when the building was handed over.[40A] Similarly the cause of action in tort arose on completion in the case of a supermarket constructed without any fire stopping, on the assumption that the building was at that date less valuable without such stopping.[40B]

[40A] [1983] 1 Const. L.J. 79, considered in *New Islington and Hackney Housing Association Limited v. Pollard Thomas and Edwards Ltd* [2001] B.L.R. 74.
[40B] *Tesco Stores Ltd v. Costain Construction Ltd* (unreported) July 2, 2003 (H.H. Judge Seymour Q.C.) at para. 250.

Latent damage.
[Add to note 50 at end: page 468]   **15–21**
See also *The Mortgage Corp v. Lambert* [2000] B.L.R. 265, CA.

[Add to note 52 at end: page 468]
See n. 36 on p. 466.

Fraud, concealment or mistake.
[Amend note 54: page 468]   **15–23**
Kleinwort Benson Ltd v. Lincoln C.C. is now reported at [1999] 2 A.C. 349,
HL.

[Add to note 55 at end: page 468]
The law on deliberate concealment is the subject of recent authority which
overrules a number of decisions since the last edition and effectively
restores the position set out in the text. Section 32 deprives a defendant of a
limitation defence in two situations: (i) where he takes active steps to
conceal his own breach of duty after he has become aware of it; and (ii)
where he is guilty of deliberate wrongdoing and conceals or fails to disclose
it in circumstances where it is unlikely to be discovered for some time.
Section 32 however does not deprive a defendant of a limitation defence for
failure to disclose a negligent breach of duty of which he was unaware of
committing—see *Cave v. Robinson Jarvis and Rolf (a firm)* [2003] 1 A.C. 384,
HL, reversing the decision of the Court of Appeal [2002] 1 W.L.R. 581 and
overruling *Brocklesby v. Armitage and Guest* [2001] 1 W.L.R. 598, CA.

Amendments.
[Add to note 73 at end: page 470]   **15–28**
On whether a claim for a new remedy is a new claim for the purposes of an
amendment, see *Lloyds Bank v. Rogers (No.2)* [1999] 3 E.G.L.R. 83.

[Add to note 74 at end: page 470]
The same facts and matters include facts and matters raised by the
defendant but not the claimant in his original claim—see *Goode v. Martin*
[2002] 1 W.L.R. 1828, CA.

[Add to note 76 at end: page 471]
See also *Darlington Building Society v. O'Rourke James Scourfield & McCarthy*
(unreported) November 3, 1998, CA; *Latreefers Inc v. Hobson* (unreported)
July 25, 2002 (Morritt V.-C.).

[Add to note 80 at end: page 471]
Where the matter is heavily documented, as is often the case in construction litigation, prejudice may be difficult to establish: *Royal Brompton
v. Hammond (No 2)* 69 Con. L.R. 132 at 143.

5–29 [Add to note 86 at end: page 472]
The new party may be a separate and unrelated party meeting a particular description—*Horne Roberts v. Smithkline Beecham Plc* [2002] 1 W.L.R. 1662, CA.

[Add to note 87 at end: page 472]
See also *Merrett v. Babb* [2001] Q.B. 1174, CA.

5. BUILDING ACT 1984 AND THE BUILDING REGULATIONS

15–31 [Delete the sentence commencing "The current consolidating statute is. . ." and replace with the following text: pages 472–473]
The current consolidating statute is the Building Act 1984 and the principal Building Regulations are the Building Regulations 2000 (S.I. 2000 No. 2531) which came into force January 1, 2001. These in turn have been amended by the Building (Amendment) Regulations 2001 (S.I. 2001 No. 3335) and the Building (Amendment) Regulations 2002 (S.I. 2002 No. 440) which came into force on April 1, 2002. Further amendments have been made by the Building (Amendment) (No. 2) Regulations 2002 (S.I. 2002 No. 2871) and the Building (Amendment) Regulations (S.I. 2003 No. 2692) which come into force on various dates in 2003 and 2004. The Regulations make substantive amendments to sections 18–21 and 59 of the Building Act 1984. Transitional provisions are contained in regulation 23 and the amending regulations contain further transitional provisions.

[Replace text of note 94 as follows: page 473]
See generally Knight, "Building Regulations 2000"; *The Building regulations explained and illustrated* (Powell-Smith, Vincent and Billington, M.J. ed., 11th ed. 1999); Stephenson, *Building Regulations Explained* (6th ed., 2000); Polley, *Understanding the Building Regulations* (2nd ed., 2000);

[Add to note 95 at end: page 473]
For details of regulations made under this section see Knight, *Building Control Law* at pp. A2–3 to A2–6.

15–32 [Delete reference to pp. 280 *et seq.* at note 98 and replace with the following: page 473]
pp. A5–2 to A5–5.

Supervision.
15–34 [Delete reference to "reg. 14" in note 3: page 474]
The relevant regulation is now reg. 15, but see also reg. 12.

[Add to note 4 at end: page 474]
This scheme is now governed by the Building (Approved Inspectors) etc Regulations 2000 (S.I. 2000 No. 2532) as amended by the Building

(Approved Inspectors), etc. (Amendment) Regulations 2001 (S.I. 2001 No. 3336) and the Building (Approved Inspectors), etc. (Amendment) Regulations 2002 (S.I. 2000 No. 2872).

Civil liability of builder.
[Add to note 12 at end: page 475]   **15–37**
A similar obligation is now contained in cl. 6.1 of the JCT 1998 Standard Form.

[Add to note 15 at end: page 475]
Clause 6.1.5 of the 1998 Form provides that the contractor is not liable to the employer for breach of statutory requirements as long as he has given notice that the employer's requirements diverge from the relevant statutory requirements—see p. 635.

6. INSOLVENCY ACT 1986

(a) Insolvency generally
[Add new note 22A at end of first sentence in the first paragraph: page 477] **15–40**
The Insolvency Act 1986 is now amended by the Insolvency Act 2000 and the Enterprise Act 2002, Pt 10.

[Delete reference to Williams and Hunter on *Bankruptcy* in note 23: page 477]

Vesting of property.
[Delete reference to Muir Hunter on *Personal Insolvency* in note 33: page **15–42** 478]

Administration.
[Add to note 37 at end: page 479]   **15–43**
See also, particularly in the context of statutory adjudication, *A. Straume (UK) Ltd v. Bradlor Developments Ltd* [2000] T.C.L.R. 409 and *Joinery Plus Ltd (in administration) v. Laing Ltd* [2003] B.L.R. 184.

(b) Insolvency of contractor

Disclaimer.
[Delete reference to Williams and Hunter on *Bankruptcy* in note 44: page **15–45** 479]

The power of sub-contractors.
[In the sentence commencing after note 66 the phrase "the bankruptcy of **15–50** winding-up of the contractor" should be corrected to "the bankruptcy *or* winding-up of the contractor": page 482]

Assignees.

15–52 [Add to note 82 at end: page 183]

In *Smith (Administrator of Cosslett (Contractors) Ltd.) v. Bridgend County Borough Council* [2002] 1 A.C. 336, the House of Lords held that an employer's right under the ICE Conditions of Contract to retain the contractor's plant on the contractor abandoning the contract is a floating charge which has to be registered under s.395 of the Companies Act 1985 if it is to be effective.

[Amend note 84 to delete reference to paragraphs 3–386 to 3–388/3 and substitute paragraph 3–2700: page 484]

[Insert new Section after paragraph 15–54: page 484]

7. PARTY WALL ETC. ACT 1996

15–55 Prior to the Party Wall, etc., Act 1996, there were a number of different principles applicable to party walls across England and Wales. London was governed by a series of Building Acts, the latest being Part VI of the London Building Acts (Amendment) Act 1939 ("the 1939 Act"). Other parts of the country (including Bristol) were governed by local acts. The majority of the country, however, was not governed by statute at all but by a complex system of common law dependent on the type of party wall under consideration. The Party Wall etc. Act came into force on July 1, 1997.[90] The 1939 Act and other local Acts were repealed at the same time.[91] The whole of England and Wales is now governed by the statutory scheme in the Party Wall etc. Act which is very similar to the previous London scheme.

15–56 The purpose of the Act is twofold. First, it allows an owner (the Building Owner) to carry out works to a party structure or to make use of a party structure. Without the sanction of the Act, some of these works would constitute a nuisance and/or a trespass. Secondly, it provides safeguards to the Adjoining Owner where works are carried out to a party structure. Prior to the Act, an adjoining owner could have been left without a remedy, for example, in a situation where the removal of the building owner's half of the party wall left his half exposed to the weather.[92] Safeguards provided include requirements to give notice to Adjoining Owners prior to carrying out any works and to make good damage caused.

15–57 The Act provides for three types of work:

(1) Construction of party structures on or at a boundary where there is no existing party structure (section 1);

---

[90] Party Wall etc. Act 1996 (Commencement) Order 1997, S.I. 1997 No. 670.
[91] Party Wall etc. Act (Repeal of Local Enactments) Order 1997, S.I. 1997 No. 671.
[92] See *Phipps v. Pears* [1965] 1 Q.B. 76. This problem has been resolved by s. 2(n) of the Act. See also *Rees v. Skerrett* [2001] 1 W.L.R. 1541 at 1553 to 1554.

(2) Works to existing party structures (section 2); and
(3) Excavations within six metres of other buildings or structures (section 6).

(a) Party walls and party structures

Although reference is generally made to party walls, the Act deals with **15–58** three types of structures: party walls, party fence walls and party structures. These are all defined in section 20.

Party walls. A party wall is either: **15–59**

  (a) a wall which forms part of a building and stands on lands of different owners to a greater extent than the projection of any artificially formed support on which the wall rests; or
  (b) so much of a wall not being a wall referred to in paragraph (a) above as separates buildings belonging to different owners.

A party wall therefore always forms part of one or more buildings. A wall **15–60** which does not stand on the land of both owners is only a party wall to the extent that it separates two buildings (subsection (b)). If a wall separates two terraced houses for two storeys of its height, but is simply the wall of one building at the third storey, it will not be a party wall at that level (unless it stands on the lands of both owners). Likewise, a wall which separates houses for the full depth of one house but then continues back as the external wall of one house only will not be a party wall beyond the end of the second house (again, unless it stands on the lands of both owners).[93]

Party fence walls. A party fence wall does not form part of a building. It is **15–61** a wall used or constructed for separating the land of two owners and which stands on the land of both owners.

Party structures. A party structure is defined as a party wall and also a **15–62** floor partition or other structure separating buildings or parts of buildings approached solely by separate staircases or entrances.

Boundary walls. Boundary walls are referred to in the Act although not **15–63** defined. It appears from the slightly complicated explanations in sections 1(1)(b) and 2(1) that a boundary wall can be either a party fence wall, the external wall of a building (both mentioned in those subsections), or a freestanding wall which only stands on the land of one party.

(b) Building Owners and Adjoining Owners

Building Owner, Adjoining Owner and Owner are all defined in section 20. **15–64** The Building Owner is an owner of land who wishes to exercise rights under the Act. The Adjoining Owner is any owner of land, buildings,

---

[93] *London, Gloucestershire and North Hants Dairy Co. v. Morley & Lanceley* [1911] 2 K.B. 257; *Drury v. Army & Navy Auxiliary Cooperative Supply Ltd.* [1896] 2 Q.B. 271.

storeys or rooms adjoining those of the Building Owner. The definition of Owner is non-exhaustive. It includes:

(a) A person in receipt of, or entitled to receive, the whole or part of the rents or profits of land;

(b) A person in possession of land, otherwise than as a mortgagee or as a tenant from year to year or for a lesser term or as a tenant at will[94]; and

(c) A purchaser of an interest in land under a contract for purchase or under an agreement for a lease, otherwise than under an agreement for a tenancy from year to year or for a lesser term.

(c) Serving of notices

15–65 One of the main safeguards of the Act is the requirement that notice must be served[95] prior to commencement of the works.[96] The notice procedures (and other safeguards for the protection of the Adjoining Owner, such as the written appointment of surveyors) must be scrupulously followed.[97] Proper compliance with the safeguards is important as the Act gives a Building Owner a statutory right to interfere with the proprietary rights of the Adjoining Owner without his consent and despite his protests.[98]

15–66 A Building Owner must serve notice on every Adjoining Owner, except that where there is a class of owners with the same interest, such as joint tenants, only one of the class need receive notice.[99] On the other hand, it seems that a notice served by a Building Owner will only be valid if served by or on behalf of both joint tenants.[1] A notice was invalidly served where it was served on the Adjoining Owner and not his surveyor in circumstances where the surveyor had not been held out as having the authority to receive service.[2] The notice must state the particulars of the work proposed clearly and intelligibly.[3]

---

[94] Similar wording in the 1939 Act was held to be limited to those who held legal interests in land of a greater duration than a yearly tenancy and to exclude statutory tenants: *Frances Holland School v. Wassef* [2001] 2 E.G.L.R. 88

[95] Methods of service are set out in s. 15

[96] See s. (d) below for the specific notices to be given for the three types of work envisaged by the Act

[97] *Gyle-Thompson v. Wall Street (Properties) Ltd.* [1974] 1 All E.R. 295 at 303. Brightman J. stated at p. 303 that he was not concerned with whether any irregularity could be waived or cured by estoppel. It is submitted that defects could be cured in appropriate cases.

[98] *Per* Brightman J. in *Gyle-Thompson v. Wall Street (Properties) Ltd.* [1974] 1 All E.R. 295 at 302.

[99] *Crosby v. Alambra Co. Ltd.* [1907] 1 Ch. 295.

[1] *Lehmann v. Herman* [1993] 1 E.G.L.R. 172. This does not mean that every person in every "layer of ownership" (*i.e.* freehold, leasehold, etc.) must serve notice: a Building Owner must be the person(s) (or layer) desirous of carrying out the works—see *Lehmann v. Herman* and *Loost v. Kremer* (unreported) May 12, 1997.

[2] *Gyle-Thompson v. Wall Street (Properties) Ltd* [1974] 1 All E.R. 295 at 303.

[3] *Hobbs, Hart v. Grover* [1899] 1 Ch. 11.

(d) The works permitted by the Act

The three types of works which the Act contemplates are set out in sections **15–67**
1, 2 and 6.

Where there is no existing party wall or party fence wall. Section 1 **15–68**
applies where there is no existing party wall or party fence wall. This
covers situations in which either the boundary is not built on at all,[4] or
where there is a wall standing on the land of one owner only and which is
not the external wall of a building.[5]

Two types of work are envisaged by section 1. First, the building owner **15–69**
may wish to build a wall which stands on both lands, *i.e.* a party wall or
party fence wall (section 1(2)). Secondly, the building owner may wish to
build a wall wholly on his own land (section 1(5)).

Notice needs to be served[6] on the Adjoining Owner at least one month **15–70**
before the Building Owner intends to start building either type of wall.[7] A
Building Owner can only build a wall standing on both lands with the
consent of the Adjoining Owner.[8] If consent is not given, he can only build
a wall wholly on his own land.[9] Nonetheless, a wall built wholly on his own
land may have footings and foundations under the Adjoining Owner's
land.[10] A wall built wholly on the Building Owner's land must be built at
his own expense.[11] When a wall is built on both lands, the expense is
shared between the two owners depending on the use they make of it.[12]

Where there is an existing party structure. Section 2 essentially applies **15–71**
where there is an existing party structure. It also covers certain works to
external walls of buildings;[13] and arches or other structures connecting
buildings.[14]

Section 2 provides a Building Owner with the right to carry out work to **15–72**
party structures where they are defective, in disrepair or do not conform to
statutory requirements (subsections (a)—(d)); and where the Building
Owner wishes to carry out works on his own account which require

---

[4] See s. 1(a).
[5] See s. 1(b).
[6] The methods by which service of a notice can be effected are set out in s. 15.
[7] See s. 1(2) and (5).
[8] See s. 1(4).
[9] See s. 1(4)(b).
[10] See s. 1(6).
[11] See s. 1(7).
[12] See s. 1(3).
[13] See s. 2(2)(a), (g) and (j).
[14] See s. 2(2)(d).

alteration to a party structure. The works falling into the latter category include underpinning (subsection (a)); cutting away projections from the wall (subsections (g) and (h)) and cutting into the wall (subsections (f) and (j)); raising the height of the wall (subsection (a)); or reducing its height (subsection (m)) unless the Adjoining Owner requires him not to do so (in accordance with section 11(7)).

15–73   Notices for works to existing party structures are dealt with in sections 3–5 of the Act. The Building Owner must serve a party structure notice[15] at least two months before work is to commence. An Adjoining Owner may serve a counter notice requiring certain works, *e.g.* chimney breasts, to be added to the Building Owner's works[16] or if he wishes certain additional work to be carried out to "special foundations" which the Building Owner wishes to build.[17] If the Adjoining Owner or the Building Owner does not consent in writing to the party structure notice or counter notice, as the case may be, within 14 days, a dispute is deemed to have arisen and must be dealt with under section 10.[18]

15–74 Work within six metres of other buildings/structures. Section 6 applies to works to be carried out on the Building Owner's own land but which, due to the depth of the foundations, may adversely affect the Adjacent Owner's building or structure. The wording is complex but, in effect, there are two situations to which the section applies:

> (1) The Building Owner wishes, within three metres of the Adjoining Owner's building, to carry out any excavation deeper than the bottom of the Adjoining Owner's foundations[19]; and
> (2) The Building Owner wishes, between three and six metres from the Adjoining Owner's building, to excavate to a depth below the bottom of the Adjoining Owner's foundations which exceeds the distance between the proposed excavation and any part of the Adjoining Owner's buildings.[20]

In both cases, the Building Owner must serve notice[21] at least one month before starting excavation.[22] The Building Owner may be required to carry out underpinning or works to strengthen or safeguard the Adjoining

---

[15] The methods by which service of a notice can be effected are set out in s. 15.

[16] See s. 4(1)(a).

[17] See s. 4(1)(b). Special foundations can only be constructed by agreement between the parties (see s. 7(4)) and are defined as foundations in which an assemblage of beams or rods is employed to distribute load (see s. 20).

[18] See s. 5.

[19] See s. 6(1).

[20] See s. 6(2).

[21] The methods by which service of a notice can be effected are set out in s. 15.

[22] See s. 6(5).

Owner's foundations.[23]. If the Adjoining Owner does not serve a notice consenting to the Building Owner's proposals within 14 days of service of the latter's notice, a dispute is deemed to have arisen and is dealt with by the surveyor(s) under section 10.[24]

(e) Dispute resolution under the Act

Disputes will either specifically arise between the parties or will be deemed **15–75** to arise when a party served with a notice does not consent within 14 days.[25] In all such cases of dispute, section 10 provides for an award to be produced by one or more surveyors. That award is final and conclusive subject to the rights of appeal in section 10(17).

There are two different procedures under section 10. Firstly, the parties **15–76** may agree on the appointment of one surveyor. Alternatively, there is a three-surveyor procedure in which each party appoints his own surveyor and the two surveyors then select a third. Appointments and selections must be in writing.[26] It is essential that the parties appoint their surveyors properly in writing or there is a real risk that any award made will be invalid.[27]

The agreed surveyor procedure. The agreed surveyor's appointment **15–77** cannot be rescinded by either party.[28] However, in the following circumstances a new surveyor can be appointed: the agreed surveyor refuses to act, he neglects to act for 10 days after a request is served on him by either of the parties, he dies, or he becomes or deems himself incapable of acting.[29] Since the parties cannot rescind an appointment, it is submitted that becoming incapable of acting must mean more than incompetence perceived by the parties. It is suggested that this would be likely to cover matters such as physical or mental illness rendering him incapable of acting.

The three-surveyor procedure. Under this system, each party must **15–78** appoint his own surveyor in writing. In default of appointment by one party, the other party can make the appointment on his behalf.[30] The two surveyors then select a third surveyor in writing "forthwith".[31]

---

[23] See s. 6(3).
[24] See s. 6(7).
[25] See ss. 5 and 6(7).
[26] See s. 10(2).
[27] *Gyle-Thompson v. Wall Street (Properties) Ltd* [1974] 1 All E.R. 295 where a surveyors' award was invalid on a number of grounds including the failure of the plaintiffs to appoint their surveyor in writing (under the equivalent provision of the 1939 Act).
[28] See s. 10(2).
[29] See s. 10(3).
[30] See s. 10(4).
[31] See s. 10(1)(b).

15–79   As with the agreed surveyor, the parties cannot rescind the appointment of their own surveyors.[32] A party may only appoint a new surveyor if the first surveyor dies, becomes or deems himself incapable of acting.[33] Unlike the agreed surveyor procedure, in this procedure, neglect or refusal to act does not lead to replacement of a surveyor. Instead, if one party's surveyor either neglects (for a period of 10 days after service of a request on him) or refuses to act effectively, the other party's surveyor is entitled to act *ex parte*. The power to act *ex parte* appears to include the power to make an *ex parte* award.[34] This would lead to a surprising result in circumstances where a third surveyor has already been appointed since, instead of an *ex parte* award, the two remaining surveyors could make an award as contemplated by section 10(10). The word "effectively" does not appear in the agreed surveyor procedure (nor did it appear in the 1939 Act). It will not be a straightforward matter for the other surveyor to decide what conduct amounts to a refusal or neglect to act effectively. If the other party's surveyor mistakenly decides that a surveyor has refused or neglected to act effectively, any consequent *ex parte* award will, it is submitted, be invalid.[35] The third surveyor can be replaced in the same circumstances as an agreed surveyor.[36] His replacement is selected by the other two surveyors.

15–80   **The award.** Where an agreed surveyor is appointed, he determines the dispute by award.[37] Where the three-surveyor procedure is used, the award can be made by all three or any two of the surveyors[38] or, where either party or either party's surveyor calls on him to do so, by the third surveyor alone.[39] In addition, as discussed at paragraph [15–79] above, if one of the two surveyors refuses or neglects to act effectively, the other surveyor may make an *ex parte* award.

15–81   By section 10(10), the surveyors are entitled to determine by award any matter connected with any work to which the Act relates and which is in dispute between the Building Owner and the Adjoining Owner. In accordance with section 10(12), the award may determine:

---

[32] See s. 10(2).

[33] See s. 10(5) and the discussion in relation to becoming incapable at para. 15–77 above.

[34] Subsections 10(6) and (7) empower the second surveyor to act "as if he had been an agreed surveyor". See also *Frances Holland School v. Wassef* [2001] 2 E.G.L.R. 88 in which the power to issue an *ex parte* award was not questioned, although the award was found to be invalid.

[35] See *Frances Holland School v. Wassef* [2001] 2 E.G.L.R. 88 (a decision under the 1939 Act which did not contain the word "effectively") in which the second surveyor's *ex parte* award was found to be invalid as it did not accurately express the grounds on which the surveyor purported to rely in order to act *ex parte* and there was no evidence to support a refusal or neglect to act by the other surveyor.

[36] See s. 10(9).

[37] See s. 10(10).

[38] See s. 10(10).

[39] See s. 10(11).

(a) The right to execute any work;

(b) The time and manner of executing any work; and

(c) Any other matter arising out of or incidental to the dispute including the costs of making the award.

The wording of sections 10(10) and 10(12)(c) appears wide. However, in **15–82** *Woodhouse v. Consolidated Property Corporation Ltd*,[40] the Court of Appeal decided that the equivalent sections in the 1939 Act had to be read in context. The dispute resolution provisions related only to resolution of differences between adjoining owners as to whether one of them should be permitted under the Act to carry out works in the relevant notice and, if so, the terms and conditions under which he was permitted to carry out such works. The award and the surveyors' powers were therefore similarly limited and the surveyors were not entitled to determine other disputes between the parties. In that case, the party wall notice was served after works had started. Before the time for consent had expired, the wall collapsed. The third surveyor determined in his award the responsibility for the collapse. This was not a matter which he was empowered to decide under the Act.

(f) Remedies

Challenging the award—appeal. The award is conclusive subject to the **15–83** parties' rights to appeal to the County Court within 14 days from the date of service.[41] It is submitted that the Court has no jurisdiction to extend this time limit since it is a statutory time limit.[42] It is also thought that the appeal constitutes a complete re-hearing.[43]

Challenging the award—invalidity. The provision that the award is **15–84** conclusive, subject to an appeal, does not prevent a challenge on the basis of invalidity.[44] Invalidity could arise where the notice has not been properly served,[45] where the surveyor was not properly appointed,[46] where the award interferes with an easement[47] or where the award is made in excess of

---

[40] [1993] 1 E.G.L.R. 174.

[41] See s. 10(16) and (17).

[42] This point was conceded in *Riley Gowler Ltd. v. National Heart Hospital Board of Governors* [1968] 3 All E.R. 1401, CA.

[43] See *Chartered Society of Physiotherapy v. Simmonds Church Smiles* 73 B.L.R. 130, a case decided in relation to similar wording in the 1939 Act and in which it was decided that the re-hearing could include evidence which was and could not have been provided to the surveyors.

[44] *Gyle-Thompson v. Wall Street (Properties) Ltd* [1974] 1 All E.R. 295 at 302; In *Re Stone and Hastie* [1903] 2 K.B. 463, CA.

[45] *Gyle-Thompson v. Wall Street (Properties) Ltd* [1974] 1 All E.R. 295—notice served on party's surveyor and not the owner.

[46] *Gyle-Thompson v. Wall Street (Properties) Ltd* [1974] 1 All E.R. 295 — surveyor not appointed in writing.

[47] See s. 9. Nothing in the Act authorises interference with easements.

jurisdiction.[48] It is submitted that, where part of an award is made in excess of jurisdiction and can be severed from the remainder, the rest of the award will remain binding.[49] In order to prevent works going ahead on the basis of an invalid award, a party may need to commence proceedings for an injunction.

15–85 Remedies where works are not carried out in accordance with the Act. A Building Owner who complies with the Act is not liable in nuisance as the Adjoining Owner's rights are supplanted by the Act, although he may incur liabilities under the statute which did not exist at common law.[50] However, where the Building Owner has failed to carry out the works in accordance with the Act, for example, by failing to serve notice prior to starting works or carrying out unauthorised works, the Adjoining Owner can rely on his rights at common law.[51] Hence, the Adjoining Owner will be able to claim damages for nuisance, trespass, negligence and/or loss of support in an appropriate case.[52] An aggrieved owner may (also) wish to seek an injunction to prevent work continuing in contravention of the Act and/or until the Building Owner has complied with the Act or, if appropriate, a mandatory injunction for the removal of unauthorised work.[53]

(g) Rights and obligations incidental to the works

15–86 Damage. There are specific provisions in section 2 of the Act which require the Building Owner to make good any damage caused to the adjoining premises, furnishings[54] and decorations as a result of the authorised works. An Adjoining Owner is entitled to claim payment of the costs

---

[48] *Woodhouse v. Consolidated Property Corporation Ltd* [1993] 1 E.G.L.R. 174, CA—surveyor determined responsibility for collapse of party wall; *Leadbetter v. Corporation of Marylebone (No. 1)* [1904] 2 K.B. 893; In *Re Stone and Hastie* [1903] 2 K.B. 463 at 474.

[49] *Selby v. Whitbread* [1917] 1 K.B. 736 at 747–8 — although the Judge treated the award as if it were an arbitration award (as to which para. 15–90 below).

[50] *Louis v. Sadiq* (1997) 74 P. & C.R. 325 at 333, CA. See also *Selby v. Whitbread* [1917] 1 K.B. 736 at 752. See also s. 7 for compensation under the Act.

[51] *Louis v. Sadiq* (1997) 74 P. & C.R. 325 at 331, 333, CA.

[52] See, *e.g. Woodhouse v. Consolidated Property Corporation Ltd* [1993] 1 E.G.L.R. 174, CA; *Louis v. Sadiq* [1997] 74 P. & C.R. 325, CA.

[53] See, *e.g. Daniells v. Mendonca* (1999) 78 P. & C.R. 401, CA—extension built without compliance with the 1939 Act; work was inadequate structurally and a trespass; mandatory injunction to remove the encroaching part of the extension. *Louis v. Sadiq* (1997) 74 P. & C.R. 325, CA—interlocutory injunction had been granted restraining further work in breach of the 1939 Act; *London and Manchester Assurance Co. Ltd. v. O and H Construction Ltd.* [1989] 2 E.G.L.G. 185—mandatory interlocutory injunction to remove structures built in breach of the 1939 Act.

[54] "Furnishings" has been substituted for "finishings" which was used in the 1939 Act. Under that Act, it was held that damage to electronic equipment, which was a chattel not a fixture, was not covered by the provision for making good damage to "the adjoining premises or to the internal finishings or decorations thereof": *Video London Sound Studios Ltd v. Asticus (GMS) Ltd* (unreported) March 6, 2001.

of making good rather than allow the Building Owner to carry out the repairs.[55] More general requirements are also set out in section 7: the Building Owner may not cause unnecessary inconvenience to Adjoining Owners and Occupiers and must compensate Adjoining Owners and Occupiers for any loss and damage caused by the works.[56]

Security. An Adjoining Owner may serve a notice requiring security from the Building Owner prior to work commencing.[57] This will be determined by the surveyors in default of agreement. Security may also be sought by the Building Owner[58] if (a) the Adjoining Owner has required some additional work to be carried out for which he will be obliged to pay[59]; or (b) if an Adjoining Owner has made a request for security from the Building Owner. No factors for determining whether security should be paid and, if so, the amount of such security are set out in the Act. It is submitted that the costs which the Adjoining Owner is likely to have to bear if the Building Owner does not complete the works properly or at all must be a highly relevant factor in determining the amount of security to be paid by the Building Owner. Where the Adjoining Owner has requested additional works, the Building Owner will obviously want reassurance that payment for such works can be made and this should be reflected in the security. Where the Building Owner asks for security simply because the Adjoining Owner has done so, it is difficult to see why security should be given or how the appropriate amount should be determined. **15–87**

Rights of entry. In order to carry out works to a party structure, the Building Owner, his contractors and surveyor are likely to need access to the adjoining property. A surveyor may need access to either property for the purpose of determining the disputes between the parties. Rights of entry are provided in section 8. Knowingly refusing to permit the exercise of these rights is a criminal offence.[60] **15–88**

Payment for the works. In the main, the costs of carrying out the work are to be borne by the Building Owner.[61] The Adjoining Owner may be required to contribute where a new party wall is built on the land of both parties[62]; where work is done to the party wall due to defects[63]; and where **15–89**

---

[55] See s.11(8).
[56] s. 7(2) changes the law from the position in *Adams v. Marylebone Borough Council* [1907] 2 K.B. 822. See also the provision at s. 1(7) for compensation for loss and damage caused to the Adjoining Owner and Occupier where the wall is constructed wholly on the Building Owner's land; and s. 11(6) for compensation for disturbance and inconvenience where premises are laid open during works under s. 2(2)(e).
[57] See s. 12(1).
[58] See s. 12(2).
[59] For example, see ss. 4(1) and 11(9).
[60] See s. 16.
[61] See s. 11.
[62] See s. 11(3).
[63] See s. 11(4) and (5).

the Adjoining Owner asks the Building Owner to carry out additional works.[64] An Adjoining Owner can subsequently be asked to contribute if he uses work originally carried out at the Building Owner's expense.[65] The Building Owner recovers any costs which the Adjoining Owner is required to pay by serving an account[66] and, if necessary, recovering the money as a debt.[67] Disputes as to responsibility for expenses and as to accounts are determined in accordance with section 10.[68]

(h) Capacity and liability of surveyors

15–90 The Act does not identify the capacity in which the surveyors act. A number of the older cases indicated that surveyors were thought to be in the position of arbitrators.[69] More recently, the view has been expressed, *obiter*, that an award under the 1939 Act was not an arbitration award but was more in the nature of an expert determination.[70]

15–91 The Act, unlike the Arbitration Act or the Housing Grants, Construction and Regeneration Act (in the case of arbitrators and adjudicators), does not provide any specific immunity for the surveyors. Whether surveyors act as experts,[71] arbitrators or quasi-arbitrators has yet to be finally determined as has the related question of whether surveyors can be liable for negligence in connection with their functions under section 10 of the Act.

---

[64] See s. 11(7) and (9).
[65] See s. 11(11).
[66] See s. 13(1).
[67] See s. 17.
[68] See s. 11(2) and 13(2).
[69] See, *e.g.* In *Re Stone and Hastie* [1903] 2 K.B. 463; *Selby v. Whitbread* [1917] 1 K.B. 736. In *Gyle-Thompson v. Wall Street (Properties) Ltd* [1974] 1 All E.R. 295, Brightman J. referred to their "quasi-judicial" position with statutory powers and responsibilities.
[70] *Chartered Society of Physiotherapy v. Simmonds Church Smiles* 73 B.L.R. 130 at 139. The older cases do not appear to have been cited.
[71] The questions of liability and immunity of experts, arbitrators and quasi-arbitrators is beyond the scope of this book. See generally: *Sutcliffe v. Thackrah* [1974] A.C. 727, HL; *Arenson v. Casson Beckman Rutley and Co.* [1977] A.C. 405, HL; *Palacath Ltd v. Flanagan* [1985] 2 All E.R. 161.

CHAPTER 16

ARBITRATION AND ADJUDICATION

1. ALTERNATIVE METHODS OF DISPUTE RESOLUTION

[Amend note 2: page 485]   **16–02**
Brown and Marriott, *ADR Principles and Practice* (2nd ed., 1999).

[Add note at end of second sentence: page 485]
For an example of a mediation procedure, see *ICE Construction Mediation Procedure 2002.*

[Amend note 8: page 486]   **16–04**
Mustill and Boyd, *Commercial Arbitration 2001 Companion* now published; *Russell on Arbitration* (22nd ed., 2002); Bernstein *et al.*, *Handbook of Arbitration Practice* (4th ed., 2003).

3. WHAT IS AN ARBITRATION AGREEMENT?

The statutory definition.
[Add to footnote 18: page 488]   **16–10**
A clause which does not mention arbitration in terms but nonetheless refers disputes to the decision of a third party (*i.e.* "a Queens Counsel") may satisfy the requirements of s. 6 if the context is such as to support an

inference that the parties intended the decision to be final and binding: *David Wilson Homes Limited v. Survey Services Limited (in liquidation)* [2001] B.L.R. 267; 80 Con. L.R. 8; [2001] 1 All E.R. (Comm.) 499, CA.

Agreement in writing.

16–11 [Add to footnote 21: page 488]
Where the contract makes it apparent that the parties contemplated arbitration as a means of dispute resolution then the parties will be bound to refer to arbitration even though the clause might not be expressed in mandatory terms: *Mangistaumunaigaz Oil Production Association v. United World Trading Inc.* [1995] 1 Lloyd's Rep. 617 as applied in *Lobb v. Aintree* [2000] B.L.R. 65; 69 Con. L.R. 79.

Incorporation by reference.

16–12 [Add to note 23: page 489]
See now also *Owner of Cargo lately laden on board MV Delos v. Delos Shipping Limited* [2001] 1 All E.R. (Comm.) 763.

Whether the procedure is arbitration.

16–13 [Add to note 26: page 489]
And now see *David Wilson Homes Limited v. Survey Services Limited (in liquidation)* [2001] B.L.R. 267; 80 Con. L.R. 8, [2001] 1 All E.R. (Comm.) 499, CA.

4. JURISDICTION OF THE ARBITRATOR

16–19 [Add to note 49: page 491]
All defences, both positive and negative in character, will fall within the jurisdiction of an arbitrator appointed to determine the Claimant's claim: *Henry Boot Construction (UK) Limited v. Malmaison Hotel (Manchester) Limited* (2000) 70 Con. L.R. 32.

[Add to note 51: page 491]
See also *Al-Naimi (t/a Buildmaster Construction Services) v. Islamic Press Agency Inc.* [2000] 1 Lloyd's Rep. 522, CA in which it was held that a Court, on a s. 9 application, could determine that extra work had been done pursuant to a second phase of the original contract and that it was covered by the arbitration clause.

Fraud.
[Correct reference in note 87: page 495]
Belcher v. Roedean School, etc., Ltd (1901) 85 L.T. 468.

Challenge to arbitrator's jurisdiction.

16–27 [Add to note 94: page 496]

A reservation of a right to challenge the jurisdiction of the arbitrator who was to rule on his own jurisdiction was sufficient to be inconsistent with an ad hoc submission to the jurisdiction of the arbitrator: *LG Caltex Gas Co Ltd v. China National Petroleum Corp.* [2001] 1 W.L.R. 1892.

[Add new note at end of second paragraph: page 496]   **16–28**
Under s. 73(1) of the 1996 Act, a party who acknowledges the arbitration agreement before the arbitrator, but argues in the arbitration that the arbitrator lacks jurisdiction on some other ground, will not be allowed to challenge the jurisdiction of the arbitrator on the ground of there being no arbitration agreement: *Athletic Union of Constantinople v. National Basketball Association* [2002] 1 Lloyd's Rep. 305.

5. DISQUALIFICATION FOR BIAS

[Add to note 8: page 497]   **16–31**
An application to have the Arbitrator removed should be brought without delay and may be lost by the applicant continuing to participate in the proceedings when it knew or ought with reasonable diligence to have known of the facts relevant to its complaint: *Rustal Trading Limited v. Gill & Duffus S.A.* [2000] 1 Lloyd's Rep. 14.

[Add to note 10: page 497]
The test as to bias was the same for a judge and an arbitrator. It was whether viewed from the perspective of a reasonable man on all the material there was a real danger of unconscious bias on the part of the decision maker. An arbitrator's relationship with a company associated with one of the parties was the same as a relationship was with that party and could amount to bias: *AT&T Corp. v. Saudi Cable Co.* [2000] B.L.R. 293; [2000] 2 Lloyd's Rep. 127, CA.
The objective approach of a reasonable man was to be applied to the question of whether there was a real danger of bias: *Save & Prosper Pensions Limited v. Homebase Limited* [2001] L.&T.R. 11.

6. OUSTING THE JURISDICTION OF THE COURT

[Add new note at the end of the paragraph: page 499]   **16–36**
The decision in *R. Durtnell & Sons Limited v. Secretary of State for Trade & Industry* [2000] B.L.R. 321 confirms that s. 18 of the 1996 Act (failure of appointment procedure) is non mandatory and therefore the Court has a discretion as to whether to appoint an arbitrator.

7. THE RIGHT TO INSIST ON ARBITRATION

16–39 [Add to note 39: page 501]
Inco Europe Limited also reported at [2000] 1 Lloyd's Rep. 467.

Multiparty proceedings.
16–51 [Add to note 67: page 504]
Dredging & Construction Co Limited v. Delta Civil Engineering Co. Limited (No.2) (2000) 72 Con. L.R. 99.

8. ARBITRATION PROCEDURE

Offer to protect costs.
16–62 [Amend note 18: page 510]
Reference should now be to *Civil Procedure 2003*, Vol. 1, para. 31.3.40.

16–63 [Add to note 27: page 512]
Lindner Ceilings Floors Partitions Plc v. Howe Engineering Services Limited [2001] B.L.R. 90.

9. CONTROL BY THE COURT

16–68 [Substitute last sentence of note 48 with the following: page 514]
See *Civil Procedure 2003*, Vol. 2, 2E Arbitration Proceedings, Pt 62—Arbitration Claims.

Appointment of arbitrator.
16–69 [Add to note 49: page 514]
See *R. Durtnell & Sons Limited v. Secretary of State for Trade & Industry* [2002] 1 Lloyd's Rep. 275; [2000] B.L.R. 321.

Injunction to restrain arbitration proceedings.
16–73 [Amend note 71: page 516]
Russell on Arbitration (22nd ed., 2002) at para. 7–030.

Serious irregularity.
16–74 [Add to footnote 74: page 516]
A tribunal's failure to obtain the consent of the parties to discuss the case with an expert appointed by them pursuant to the powers granted by s. 37(1) of the 1996 Act amounted, on the facts, to an irregularity but not a serious irregularity as defined by s. 68(2): *Hussman (Europe) Limited v. Al Ameen Development & Trade Co.* [2000] 2 Lloyd's Rep. 83.

A serious irregularity had to pass the test of causing substantial injustice before a Court would act. S. 68 was only available in extreme cases where justice called out for corrective action by the Court. It was not to be used as a means of circumventing the restrictions on the Court's power to intervene. S. 68(2)(d) did not require the tribunal to set out each step by which they reached their conclusion or to deal with each point made by a party. An award may be remitted if the reasons do not enable the Court to consider an application under s. 69: *The Petro Ranger* [2001] 2 Lloyd's Rep. 348.

[Add new note at the end of paragraph (g): page 517]
S. 68(2)(g) requires a finding of unconscionable conduct on behalf of the relevant party: *Cuflet Chartering v. Carousel Shipping Co. Ltd* [2002] 1 Lloyd's Rep. 707.

Removal of an arbitrator.
[Add new note at the end of the first sentence: page 517]   16–75
The Court should not make a finding of misconduct against an arbitrator without giving him notice of the proposed grounds of such a finding. Even a finding of misconduct may not be inconsistent with a decision that the arbitrator could deal with the case fairly if it were remitted back to him. That would depend on whether a reasonable person would have lost confidence in his ability to reach a fair and balanced determination of the remitted issues: *Miller Construction Limited v. James Moore Earthmoving* [2001] 2 All E.R. (Comm.) 598, CA.

Appeals to the High Court.
[Add to note 5: page 521]   16–83
As to the scope of s. 57(3), allowing correction of a clerical mistake, see *Gannet Shipping v. Eastrade Commodities Inc.* [2002] 1 Lloyd's Rep. 713 where an arbitrator who made an accidental slip could correct it and amend a subsequent award as to costs which was based upon the slip. Use of a wrong figure was a slip if the figure was wrong and it was accidental if the arbitrator had not meant to use the wrong figure.

[Add to note 7: page 521]
For factors that may be relevant to an application to extend the time limit, see *Kalmnet JSC v. Glencore International AG* [2002] 1 All E.R. 76.

[Add to note 8: page 521]
Section 69(3)(b) is an addition to the *Nema* guidelines, reducing the difference of view between the Commercial Court and the Court of Appeal in *Petraco (Bermuda) Ltd. v. Petromed* [1988] 2 Lloyd's Rep. 357. Whilst the statutory criteria are strongly influenced by the *Nema* guidelines they do not follow them entirely. They open the door a little more widely to the granting of permission to appeal: see *CMA CGM S.A. v. Beteiligungs-Kommanditgesellschaft* [2003] 1 Lloyd's Rep. 212. These criteria apply to construction cases as to any other case.

16–84 [Substitute second sentence of text with the following: page 521]
The detailed procedure and evidential requirements are set out in Civil
Procedure 2003, Vol. 2, Arbitration Proceedings, Pt 62, Arbitration Claims
and the Practice Direction—Arbitration, para. 2E-41. Specifically, para. 12
of the Practice Direction deals with applications for permission (leave) to
appeal.

[Add to note 10: page 521]
and see para. 12.4 of the Practice Direction—Arbitration (Civil Procedure
2003, Vol. 2, para. 2E-41).

16–85 [Add additional first sentence: page 521]
An arbitration claim, including an application for permission to appeal
from an arbitrator's award may, if the subject matter is appropriate, be
issued in the Technology & Construction Court List: see para. 2 of the
Practice Direction—Arbitration (Civil Procedure 2003, Vol. 2, para. 2E-41).

[Add at end of paragraph: page 521]
No appeal lies to the Court of Appeal without the permission of the Court
below against a decision under s. 69 of the Act: *Henry Boot Construction
(UK) Limited v. Malmaison Hotel (Manchester) Limited* [2001] Q.B. 388, CA.
Further, should the Court decide to refuse an application for permission to
appeal, it need only give the briefest of reasons in order to comply with s. 6
of the Human Rights Act 1996. In appropriate cases the reasons might be
no more than a statement of which of the threshold tests in s. 69(3) the
applicant had failed to demonstrate: *North Range Shipping Limited v.
Seatrans Shipping Corp* [2002] 2 Lloyd's Rep. 1, CA.

Refusal to enforce award.
16–88 [Add to note 28: page 523]
In respect of a New York Convention Award, enforcement may be refused
in the circumstances outlined in s. 103(2) of the 1996 Act, including
circumstances in which the arbitrator had arguably conducted the arbitration in breach of natural justice such that the party resisting enforcement
was to be regarded as having been unable to present his case: s. 103(2)(c) of
the 1996 Act and *Irvani v. Irvani* [2000] 1 Lloyd's Rep. 412, CA.

[Add to note 31: page 523]
Good Challenger Navigante S.A. v. Metalexportimport S.A. [2003] 1 Lloyd's
Rep. 71.

10. INTERNATIONAL ARBITRATION UNDER ICC RULES

Appointment of arbitrators.
16–92 [Add to note 59: page 526]

The jurisdiction of the High Court is not excluded by the finality provisions of the ICC Rules, but where the Court considered that there was no case of common law bias, it was unreasonable to hold that the arbitrator lacked the independence required by the ICC Rules: *AT&T Corp. v. Saudi Cable Co.* [2000] B.L.R. 293; [2000] 2 Lloyd's Rep. 127, CA.

11. ADJUDICATION UNDER STATUTE

[Replace existing paragraphs 16–100 to 16–118: pages 530 to 536 with the following text]

Statutory adjudication. Section 108 of the Housing Grants Construction and Regeneration Act 1996[4] introduced, for the first time, a mandatory dispute resolution procedure in the field of construction contracts. It has been widely accepted by the construction industry[5] as a primary means of dispute resolution, particularly in smaller monetary claims.[6] **16–100**

The requirements of the Act. Section 108 gives a party to a construction contract[7] a right to refer a dispute[8] arising under the contract to adjudication under a procedure complying with the section.[9] The minimum requirements[10] are as follows: **16–101**

(a) The contract must provide a timetable with the object of securing the appointment of the adjudicator and referral of the dispute to him within seven days of such notice.

(b) The contract must require the adjudicator to reach a decision within 28 days of referral or such longer period as is agreed by the parties after the dispute has been referred.

(c) The contract must allow the adjudicator to extend the period of 28 days by up to 14 days with the consent of the party by whom the dispute was referred (normally known as the "referring party").

(d) The contract must impose a duty on the adjudicator to act impartially.

(e) The contract must enable the adjudicator to take the initiative in ascertaining the facts and the law.

(f) The contract must provide that the decision of the adjudicator is binding until the dispute is finally determined by legal proceedings, by arbitration or by agreement.

---

[4] See para. A-05 of the 7th ed.
[5] See, for example, *Report No.5 of the Adjudication Reporting Centre* [2003] 19 Const. L.J. 269.
[6] *Report No.5 of the Adjudication Reporting Centre* [2003] 19 Const. L.J. at 276, 277.
[7] See s. 104 of the Act and paras 3–36A and 15–15C of the 7th ed. for the meaning of a construction contract.
[8] For this purpose dispute includes any difference—see s. 108(1) of the Act.
[9] s. 108(1) of the Act.
[10] s. 108(2) to (5) of the Act.

(g) The contract must also provide that the adjudicator is not liable for anything done or omitted in the discharge or purported discharge of his functions as adjudicator unless the act or omission is in bad faith, and that any employee or agent of the adjudicator is similarly protected from liability.

16–102 The Scheme. If the contract does not comply with these requirements, then the adjudication provisions of the Scheme for Construction Contracts apply.[11] The Act does not render void a non-compliant procedure and a party to such a contract could adjudicate under that contractual arrangement, but is not bound by statute to do so. That party could still insist on adjudicating under the Scheme.

12. THE APPROACH TO ADJUDICATION

16–103 Approach of the Courts. On the first occasion upon which the Courts had to consider those adjudication provisions Dyson J. said in *Macob Civil Engineering Ltd v. Morrison Construction Ltd*[12]:

"The intention of Parliament in the Act was plain. It was to introduce a speedy mechanism for settling disputes and construction contracts on a provisional interim basis, and requiring the decision of adjudicators to be enforced pending the final determination of disputes by arbitration, litigation or agreement. . . . The timetable for adjudication is very tight . . . many would say unreasonably tight, and likely to result in injustice. Parliament must have been taken to have been aware of this. . . . It is clearly Parliament's intention that the adjudication should be conducted in a manner which those familiar with the grinding detail of the traditional approach to the resolution of construction disputes apparently find it difficult to accept. But Parliament has not abolished arbitration and litigation of construction disputes. It has merely introduced an intervening provisional stage in the dispute resolution process. Crucially, it has made it clear that decisions of adjudicators are binding and are to be complied with until the dispute is finally resolved".

---

[11] See s. 108(5) of the Act at para. A-05 of the 7th ed. and Pt I of the Scheme at paras B-06 *et seq.* of the 7th ed. The extent to which the contractual mechanism does not comply with the Act is irrelevant. If it does not comply the whole contractual mechanism is tainted and falls by the wayside to be replaced by the provisions of the Scheme, see *John Mowlem Ltd v. Hydra-Tight Ltd* (2001) 17 Const. L.J. 358; [2000] C.I.L.L. 1649–1652; H.T. 00–184, QBD (TCC), where a contractual requirement for "notice of dissatisfaction" meant that the contractual mechanism fell away to be replaced by provisions of the Scheme.

[12] [1999] B.L.R. 93 at 97.

In a number of subsequent decisions the Court of Appeal has approved this **16-104** passage or has adopted a similar interpretation of the statutory adjudication process by reference to its presumed underlying purpose of the legislation.[13]

Approach of the parties. The approach of the parties to adjudication has **16-105** shown certain developments. The magnitude of legal and expert costs that parties to adjudications are incurring appears to be significant; and the adjudicator's own fees and costs are not insignificant[14] (and have been subject to judicial comment, albeit restrained[15]). This may reflect the increasing importance attributed to the adjudication proceedings and a realisation that success or failure in such proceedings is often finally determinative of the dispute. In many cases it seems that the parties are accepting the decision of the adjudicator and the number of adjudication decisions which are revisited in arbitration or the courts is small.

Particular tactics have developed in adjudication. Often the referring party **16-106** will have the advantage of a long period of preparation. If this is then followed by a reference at a period such as the traditional construction industry holidays, it can markedly affect the ability of the responding party to prepare its case, leading to so-called "ambush". Another tactic is for a number of sub-contractors to collectively decide to serve referral notices on the same main contractor at the same time. These practices can lead to a procedure which is unfair and it is suggested that adjudicators need to be alert to such tactics so that, within the limits of the procedure, they can conduct the adjudication keeping a balance between the parties and allowing both parties a proper opportunity to prepare and present their case.

13. ADJUDICATION PROCEDURE

Right to refer at any time. The courts have strictly construed the **16-107** requirement that notice can be given at any time. A provision requiring mandatory mediation prior to either party exercising the right to adjudication has been held to fetter the unqualified entitlement to adjudication and to be unenforceable[16]; as has a requirement for a notice of dissatisfaction which delayed the right of either party to refer a dispute to adjudication.[17]

---

[13] *Bouygues (United Kingdom) Ltd v. Dahl-Jensen (United Kingdom) Ltd* [2000] B.L.R. 522; *C&B Scene Concept Design Ltd v. Isobars Ltd* [2002] B.L.R. 93; and *Ferson Contractors Ltd v. Levolux A T Ltd* [2003] B.L.R. 118. For a recent critical discussion of the decision in *Macob*, see Sheridan and Helps, "What's wrong with Macob? The first decision on adjudication revisited" (2002) 18 Const. L.J. 233.
[14] See *Report No.5 of the Adjudication Reporting Centre* [2003] 19 Const. L.J. 269 at 279.
[15] See, for example, *Edmund Nuttall Ltd v. R.G. Carter Ltd* [2002] B.L.R. 312.
[16] *R.G. Carter Ltd v. Edmund Nuttall Ltd*, unreported (June 21, 2000).
[17] *John Mowlem Ltd v. Hydra-Tight Ltd*, *supra*.

Neither does a party waive or abandon its right to go to adjudication at any time if it issues court proceedings in respect of the same claims.[18] A party can give a valid notice of adjudication after determination under a contract[19] or it is submitted, by analogy, after the contract has otherwise been brought to an end.

16–108 Appointment of adjudicator. Section 108(2)(b) of the Act requires the contract to provide a timetable with the object of securing the appointment of the adjudicator and referral of the dispute to him within seven days of the adjudication notice. In practice this timetable is usually achieved. The appointment of the adjudicator is frequently carried out by an adjudicator nominating body.[20] There are now a number of standard terms for the appointment of adjudicators.[21]

16–109 Decisions as to jurisdiction. An adjudicator's jurisdiction is derived from the terms of his appointment as agreed by the parties,[22] and is accordingly a question of construction to which ordinary principles apply. The adjudicator will only have jurisdiction to determine a dispute referred to him arising out of a construction contract[23] entered into after May 1, 1998[24] and satisfying the formal requirements as to agreements in writing.[25] If any of these requirements are absent, any decision is a nullity and is not binding on the parties.[26]

16–110 The question whether the adjudicator has the necessary jurisdiction is not itself a dispute arising under a construction contract and an adjudicator has no jurisdiction to decide his own jurisdiction. Any such decision of an adjudicator on jurisdiction is not binding.[27]

16–111 As a matter of practice where the adjudicator's jurisdiction is contested it is submitted that the appropriate approach is for the adjudicator to enquire into his jurisdiction and if he is satisfied that he has jurisdiction he should continue with the adjudication unless and until the court orders other-

---

[18] *Herschel Engineering Ltd v. Breen Property Ltd* [2000] B.L.R. 272.
[19] See *A & D Maintenance Construction Ltd v. Pagehurst Construction Services Ltd* [1999] C.I.L.L. 1518.
[20] See para. 2(1) of the Scheme: para. B-07 of the 7th ed. For a list of the bodies, see *Report No.5 of the Adjudication Reporting Centre* [2003] 19 Const. L.J. 269.
[21] See, for instance, the ICE Adjudicator's Agreement under the Ajudication Procedure 1997.
[22] See *Fastrack Contractors Ltd v. Morrison Construction Ltd* [2000] B.L.R. 168; *KNS Industrial Services (Birmingham) Ltd v. Sindall Ltd* (2000) 75 Con. L.R. 71; *Edmund Nuttall Ltd v. R G Carter Ltd* [2002] B.L.R. 312; and *Joinery Plus Ltd v. Laing Ltd* [2003] B.L.R. 184 which at 195 contains a very useful distillation of the applicable principles.
[23] See s. 104 of the Act and paras 3–36A and 15–15C of the 7th ed. and see para. 16–127 below.
[24] See S.I. 1998 No. 650 and para. 15–15C of the 7th ed.
[25] s. 107 of the Act. See para. 15–15D of the 7th ed.
[26] See, *e.g. The Project Consultancy Group v. Trustees of the Gray Trust* [1999] B.L.R. 377.
[27] *Homer Burgess Ltd v. Chirex (Annan) Ltd* [2000] B.L.R. 124.

wise.[28] Where the party disputing jurisdiction sends written submissions to the adjudicator in relation to the issue of jurisdiction inviting the adjudicator to decide the issue, any decision of the adjudicator would be binding upon that party.[29] Where a party reserves its position with regard to the jurisdiction of the adjudicator, it does not thereby submit to that jurisdiction, and any decision by the adjudicator as to his jurisdiction is not binding upon that party. To the extent that the court subsequently decides that there was no jurisdiction, the decision of the adjudicator would be a nullity.[30]

Adjudication procedure. The Act requires the contract to enable the **16–112** adjudicator to take the initiative in ascertaining the facts and the law.[31] The procedure is otherwise not prescribed. The Scheme sets out detailed powers of the adjudicator[32] in cases where the Scheme applies. In many cases the parties adopt a standard procedure[33] but these often leave much of the detailed procedure to the discretion of the adjudicator. The procedure adopted by the adjudicator must comply with the rules of natural justice.[34]

The duty to act impartially. The contract must impose a duty on the **16–113** adjudicator to act impartially.[35] The Scheme obviously includes that provision.[36]

Adjudicator's decision. The Act does not provide that the contract should **16–114** contain any requirements as to the form of decision or any formalities. Neither is there any provision in the Act that the contract must require the adjudicator to give reasons. The Scheme contains no such requirements. In practice, adjudicators often adopt a form similar to an arbitration award but giving minimal reasons for the decision.

Failure to reach a decision within the time limit. The Act simply states **16–115** that the contract must require the adjudicator to reach a decision with 28 days of referral or such longer period as is agreed by the parties after the dispute has been referred.[37] The Act also requires that the contract must

---

[28] See *ABB Power Construction Ltd v. Norwest Holst Engineering Ltd* [1999] C.I.L.L. 1518 where it was stated that insofar as the adjudicator finds an arguable case that he has jurisdiction he should continue with the adjudication unless and until the court orders otherwise but note the caution that the adjudicator's approach here, although sensible and pragmatic, might not be right in another case.

[29] *Whiteways Contractors (Sussex) Ltd v. Impressa Castelli Construction U.K. Ltd* [2000] C.I.L.L. 1664.

[30] *The Project Consultancy Group v. The Trustees of the Gray Trust* [1999] B.L.R. 377.

[31] s. 108(2)(f) of the Act.

[32] paras 12 *et seq.* of the Scheme and, in particular, para. 13: see paras B-17 *et seq.* of the 7th ed.

[33] See, for instance, the ICE Adjudication Procedure 1997.

[34] See para. 16–140 and 16–141, below.

[35] s. 108(2)(e) of the Act.

[36] para. 12 of the Scheme: see para. B-17 of the 7th ed.

[37] s. 108(2)(c) of the Act.

allow the adjudicator to extend the period of 28 days by up to 14 days, with the consent of the party by whom the dispute was referred.[38] The Scheme, where it applies, states that where the adjudicator fails to reach his decision within the time limits in the Scheme, any of the parties to the dispute may serve a fresh adjudication notice and request an adjudicator to act.[39] The parties can obviously agree to extend the time limit.[40] Where the parties do not so agree and no other principle of law affects the time, then the decision is one which is not given in accordance with the contract time limits or the limits in the Scheme. There is however no requirement that, in such circumstances, the decision is of no effect.[41]

16–116 **Mistakes.** The general rule is that the adjudicator's decision will be binding if he asked the right question but answered it in the wrong way. This is subject to one qualification. It appears that where a mistake is brought to the attention of the adjudicator, or he otherwise appreciates a mistake, within a reasonable time of the publication of his decision, the adjudicator is entitled to correct the error arising from an accidental error or omission, and the courts will give effect only to the corrected decision.[42] The basis of this jurisdiction is unclear. The Scheme does not address the question of whether, and if so, in what circumstances an error can be corrected and in one case[43] the power was said to arise by way of the implied term. Where the adjudicator does not recognise or accept an error in his decision, then the decision will be enforced in the ordinary way even if obviously wrong.[44]

16–117 **Costs.** The adjudicator's jurisdiction to decide upon liability for the costs of the parties is entirely a matter of construction of the applicable contractual terms or adjudication rules, and is largely a matter of policy for the rule makers. For example, the TECBAR Adjudication Rules provide that each party should bear its own costs of the adjudication, as does the ICE Arbitration Procedure (1997), unless all parties concerned agree that the adjudicator should have discretion to award costs. In contrast, the Scheme is silent as to the adjudicator's jurisdiction to award costs of the parties, as are some of the institutional rules. In *Northern Developments (Cumbria) Limited v. J & J Nichol*[45] it was held that, absent an express power

---

[38] s. 108(2)(d) of the Act.
[39] para. 19(2)(a) of the Scheme: see para. B-24 of the 7th ed.
[40] See, for instance, para. 19(1) of the Scheme: para. B-24 of the 7th ed.
[41] See *Simons Construction Ltd. v. Aardvark Developments* Ltd, unreported (October 29, 2003) and the Scottish decision in *St Andrews Bay Development Ltd. v. HBG Management Ltd.* [2003] C.I.L.L. 2016.
[42] See *Bloor Construction (U.K.) Ltd v. Bowmer & Kirkland (London) Ltd* [2000] B.L.R. 314 and *Edmund Nuttall Ltd v. Sevenoaks District Council*, unreported (April 14, 2000).
[43] *Bloor Construction (U.K.) Ltd v. Bowmer & Kirkland (London) Ltd* [2000] B.L.R. 314.
[44] See, *e.g. Bouygues (U.K.) Ltd v. Dahl-Jensen (UK) Ltd (In Liquidation)*, [2000] B.L.R. 522.
[45] [2000] B.L.R. 158.

to award costs, the adjudicator could not award costs of the parties.[46] However, where both parties ask in writing for their costs, without submitting to the adjudicator that he has no jurisdiction to make an award in respect of those costs, then the adjudicator was granted such jurisdiction by implied agreement of the parties.[47] There is nothing objectionable to an express contractual provision which provides that the party serving the notice of adjudication should bear all of the adjudicator's costs and fees and all of the costs and expenses incurred by both parties in relation to any adjudication.[48]

Adjudicator's fees and expenses. The jurisdiction of the adjudicator to **16–118** make a decision in respect of his own fees and expenses is subject to the provisions of the construction contract, or the rules applicable to the adjudication. Most, if not all, of the standard rules, including the Scheme, permit the adjudicator to determine which party, or in what proportions the parties, should pay his fees and expenses. Notwithstanding any decision, under the Scheme and most, if not all, institutional rules, both parties are jointly and severally liable in respect of his fees and expenses reasonably incurred.[49]

14. ENFORCEMENT OF THE ADJUDICATOR'S DECISION

General approach to enforcement. The courts have taken a robust, and **16–119** purposive, attitude to enforcement of adjudicator's decisions, and will generally enforce any decision made by an adjudicator with jurisdiction to make that decision.

Basis of enforcement. It is a notable feature of the Act that, unlike the **16–120** Arbitration Act 1996, it does not make any provision for enforcement or require the contract to contain terms making such provision in a particular form.[50] Thus:

> "The decision does not have the status of a judgment, nor is there any provision in the Act corresponding to s. 66 of the Arbitration Act, under which, by leave of the court, judgment may be entered in terms of an arbitral award, or the award may be enforced in the same manner as a judgment. . ."[51]

---

[46] But see *John Cothliff Ltd v. Allen Build (North West) Ltd* [1999] C.I.L.L 1530 in which an adjudicator's decision as to costs of the parties was enforced.
[47] *Northern Developments (Cumbria) Ltd v. J & J Nichol* [2000] B.L.R. 158.
[48] *Bridgeway Construction Ltd v. Tolent Construction Ltd* [2000] C.I.L.L. 1662–1664.
[49] Para. 25 of Pt I of the Scheme, see para. B-30 of the 7th ed.
[50] See *VHE Construction plc v. RBSTB Trust Co Ltd* [2000] B.L.R. 187.
[51] *VHE Construction plc v. RBSTB Trust Co Ltd* [2000] B.L.R. 187 at 195.

16–121 **Implied obligation to comply.** The obligation upon a party to comply with a valid decision is, it seems, to be implied from the agreement of the parties to refer disputes to adjudication, coupled with the fact that the adjudicator's decision is binding in accordance with section 108(3) of the Act.[52] The Scheme, where it applies, contains an express provision that the parties shall comply with the decision until the dispute is finally determined.[53] As a contractual obligation, it raises questions as to the relationship of that obligation with other obligations under the contract.[54] If the contract is determined and the obligation to pay is suspended, that may override the contractual obligation to pay but, on the facts, may still give a right to enforce the decision.[55]

16–122 **Summary judgment.** The appropriate procedural route for enforcement is by summary judgment, and it may be necessary to seek to abridge time for acknowledgment of service of proceedings and for the service of evidence in opposition to a summary judgment application.[56] An issue which challenges the jurisdiction of the adjudicator, so long as it is reasonably and clearly raised, must be determined by the court on the balance of probabilities with, if necessary, oral and documentary evidence.[57]

16–123 **Stay of execution.** The court has given the paying party a stay of execution in a number of decided cases. However, it is necessary to differentiate between two conceptually distinct types of stay:

(1) where the successful claimant in enforcement proceedings is in liquidation, then the liquidation operates as an automatic stay of the proceedings by virtue of rule 4.90 of the Insolvency Rules 1986[58];

(2) where the successful claimant in enforcement proceedings is impecunious to the extent that, on the evidence, there are serious concerns that the claimant will not be able to repay sums claimed if the

---

[52] Compare this with the slightly different approach taken in *David McLean Housing Contractors Limited v. Swansea Housing Association Ltd* [2002] B.L.R. 125. For a discussion of this topic, see Sheridan and Helps, "The juridical basis for enforcement of adjudicators' decisions" (2003) 19 Const. L.J. 144.

[53] para. 23(2) of the Scheme: see para. B-28 of the 7th ed.

[54] See Sheridan and Helps, "Construction Act Review, Enforcement of adjudicators' decisions: competing contractual obligations" (2003) 19 Const. L.J. 193.

[55] See *Ferson Contractors Ltd. v. Levolux A.T. Ltd* [2003] EWCA Civ 11; [2003] 1 All E.R. (Comm.) 385. Although that case rejected the analysis in *Bovis Lend Lease Ltd. v. Triangle Developments* [2003] B.L.R. 31, the decision in *Ferson* could have based on the narrow grounds that the sub-contractor could suspend and the determination was wrongful.

[56] *Outwing Construction Ltd v. H. Randall & Son Ltd* [1999] B.L.R. 156 at 160 on the basis that ". . . Parliament intended that adjudicator's decisions and order, if not complied with, were to be enforced without delay."

[57] *The Project Consultancy v. The Trustees of the Gray Trust* [1999] B.L.R. 377.

[58] The effect of r. 4.90 was explained by Lord Hoffmann in *Stein v. Blake (No.1)* [1996] 1 A.C. 243 at 252; and for its application in the context of the enforcement of an adjudicator's decision, see *Bouygues (UK) Ltd v. Dahl-Jensen (UK) Ltd* [2000] B.L.R. 522, CA.

adjudicator's decision is later overturned in arbitral or court proceedings, then the court may, in the exercise of its discretion, stay the proceedings on such terms as it thinks fit, on the basis that ". . . there are special circumstances which render it inexpedient to enforce the judgment or order . . ."[59]

15. GROUNDS FOR OPPOSING ENFORCEMENT

Basis for resisting enforcement. Enforcement may be resisted on a **16–124** number of grounds and, in particular, that:

(1) there is no contract in writing;

(2) there is no "construction contract" within the meaning of the Act [60];

(3) the statutory requirements of the contract being in writing or evidenced in writing have not been met;

(4) there was no "dispute" capable of being referred to adjudication on the date of the purported referral;

(5) the adjudicator did not have jurisdiction over an issue or question or has gone outside his terms of reference[61];

(6) the adjudicator has conducted the adjudication so as to breach the principles of natural justice so seriously that the purported decision ought not to be enforced;

(7) there has been a breach of the European Convention on Human Rights;

(8) the adjudication provision does not, by operation of law, bind one party. This may be the position in the case of a consumer, by operation of the Unfair Terms in Consumer Contracts Regulations 1999[62];

---

[59] *Herschel Engineering Limited v Breen Properties Ltd* [2000] B.L.R. 272 (Dyson J.); *Rainford House Ltd v. Cadogan Ltd* [2001] B.L.R. 416. However, it will always be necessary for the Court to give sufficient weight to the competing right of the claimant to have his decision enforced (*Baldwins Industrial Services plc (in administrative receivership) v. Barr Ltd* [2003] B.L.R. 176) so that a Court is unlikely to grant a stay on limited or flimsy evidence of impecuniosity (*Absolute Rentals Ltd v. Gencor Enterprises Ltd* [2000] C.I.L.L. 1637). The test to be applied under s. 726(1) of the Companies Act 1985 in relation to security for costs may be a helpful analogy: *Herschel Engineering Ltd v. Breen Properties Ltd* (*supra*); *Rainford House Ltd v. Cadogan Ltd* [2001] B.L.R. 416. *RSL (South West) Ltd v. Stansell* [2003] C.I.L.L. 2012.
[60] *The Project Consultancy Group v. The Trustees of the Gray Trust* [1999] B.L.R. 377.
[61] *Bouygues, supra.*
[62] *Picardi v. Cuniberti* (2003) 19 Const. L.J. 350 , although see *Lovell Projects Ltd v. Legg and Carver* [2003] C.I.L.L. 2019 which distinguishes *Picardi* on the facts.

16–125 Valid decisions. There are also various grounds which cannot be used to challenge the enforcement of a decision[63]:

(9) A decision of an adjudicator whose validity is challenged as to its factual or legal conclusions or as to procedural error remains a decision that is both enforceable and should be enforced.[64]

(10) A decision that is erroneous, even if the error is disclosed by the reasons, will still not ordinarily be capable of being challenged and should, ordinarily, still be enforced.[65]

(11) A decision which gives a mistaken answer to an issue within the adjudicator's jurisdiction.[66]

16–126 No Contract. On an application for summary judgment, enforcement will be refused if there is no contract or, arguably, no contract in writing between the parties because the adjudicator does not have jurisdiction.[67]

16–127 No "Construction Contract". Where there is no "construction contract" between the parties within the meaning of section 108 of the Act, the adjudicator does not have jurisdiction.[68] This will commonly occur if the works or the relevant works do not fall within the definition of "construction operations" to be found in sections 104 and 105 of the Act. If there is a construction contract but the terms of the contract are not readily ascertainable, the Scheme may apply.[69]

16–128 No contract in writing. Section 107 of the Act provides that the relevant part of the Act, including the provision for adjudication, only applies where the contract is in writing. There are detailed provisions as to the requirements for an agreement in writing which mirror the provisions in the Arbitration Act 1996.[70] An adjudicator has no jurisdiction where there is an oral contract nor does an adjudicator have jurisdiction to decide whether an oral agreement existed which varied the terms of a written agreement.[71]

---

[63] *Sherwood & Casson Limited v. Mackenzie Engineering Limited* [2000] C.I.L.L. 1577.

[64] *Macob v. Morrison* [1999] B.L.R. 93.

[65] *Bouygues (UK) Limited v. Dahl-Jensen (UK) Limited* [2000] B.L.R. 522.

[66] The court should give a fair, natural and sensible interpretation to the decision in the light of the disputes that are the subject of the reference: *Bouygues (UK) Limited v. Dahl-Jensen (UK) Limited* [2000] B.L.R. 522.

[67] *The Project Consultancy Group v. The Trustees of the Gray Trust* [1999] B.L.R. 377. For a discussion of the circumstances in which a party may lose the right to contend that there is no contract, see the *obiter* comments in *Maymac Environmental Services v. Faraday Building Services* [2000] C.I.L.L. 1685, QBD (TCC). See also para. 3–36C of the 7th ed.

[68] *The Project Consultancy Group v. The Trustees of the Gray Trust* [1999] B.L.R. 377.

[69] *Pegram Shopfitters Ltd v. Tally Wiejl (UK) Ltd* [2003] C.I.L.L. 1990–1992

[70] See s. 5 of the Arbitration Act 1996.

[71] *Carillion Construction Ltd v. Davenport Royal Dockyard* [2003] B.L.R. 79.

No dispute. For the adjudicator to have jurisdiction there must be a **16–129** dispute. If there is no dispute there is no jurisdiction. Section 108(1) of the Act provides that a party has the right to refer a "dispute arising under the contract" to adjudication. It also states that "dispute" includes any difference. Section 108(2)(a) provides for a notice to be given in respect of a "dispute".[72] A referring party must refer a single dispute "arising out of a single contract".[73]

Disputes "under the contract". Particular questions may arise as to **16–130** whether the dispute is one which arises "under the contract". In *Shepherd Construction Ltd v. Mecright Ltd*[74] the Court held that questions as to whether a compromise agreement was voidable for want of consideration and/or economic duress were not within the jurisdiction of an adjudication in respect of any dispute arising "under" the contract.[75] An adjudicator will ordinarily have jurisdiction to decide upon rectification of the contract.[76]

The existence of a dispute. There have been many decisions in which the **16–131** question of whether there was a dispute was raised on enforcement. Whilst much must depend on the facts of a particular case, an initial question is whether there is in principle any difference between the test in adjudication and the test that has developed over the years in arbitration.[77]

In the context of arbitration, the Court of Appeal considered the meaning of **16–132** the word "dispute" in *Halki Shipping Corp v. Sopex Oils*[78] as being any claim of which the opposing party had been notified which that party has refused to admit or not paid. This reasoning has been adopted in a number of decisions on adjudication, see *Watkin Jones & Sons v. LIDL GmbH(No.1)*[79]; *Cowlin Construction Ltd. v. CFN Architects Ltd*[80]; *Orange EBS v. ABB Ltd.*[81]

Other decisions have tended to suggest that something more elaborate is **16–133** required to crystallise a dispute for the purposes of adjudication, see *Fastrack Contractors Ltd v. Morrison Construction Ltd*[82]; *Sindall Ltd v. Sol-*

---

[72] See *Grovedeck Ltd v. Capital Demolition Ltd* [2000] B.L.R. 181 on this point.
[73] Although the Scheme allows the disputing parties to agree to extend the reference to cover "more than one dispute under the same contract" and "related disputes under different contracts"—see *Fastrack Contractors Ltd v. Morrison Construction Ltd* [2000] B.L.R. 168 at 176.
[74] [2000] B.L.R. 489, TCC.
[75] For a contrary decision distinguished on the facts see *Quarmby Construction Company Ltd v. Larraby Land Ltd*, unreported (April 14, 2003).
[76] *Christiani & Nielsen v. The Lowry Centre Development Co. Ltd*, unreported (June 28, 2000).
[77] See Sheridan and Helps, "Construction Act Review, The meaning of the word "dispute" for the purposes of s.108 of the HGCR Act 1996" (2003) 19 Const. L.J. 319.
[78] [1998] 1 W.L.R. 726.
[79] [2002] C.I.L.L. 1834–1836.
[80] [2003] B.L.R. 241.
[81] [2003] B.L.R. 323.
[82] [2000] B.L.R. 168.

land[83]; *K & D Construction Ltd v. Midas Homes Ltd*[84]; *Costain Ltd. v. Wescol Steel Ltd.*[85] and *Edmund Nuttall Ltd v. R G Carter Ltd.*[86]

16–134 In *Beck Peppiatt v. Norwest Holst,*[87] Forbes J. reiterated that questions as to the existence and nature of a dispute were matters of fact, although he endorsed the guidance provided in *Sindall Ltd v. Solland*[88]: "for there to be a dispute for the purposes of exercising the statutory right to adjudication it must be clear that a point has emerged from the process of discussion or negotiation that has ended and that there is something which needs to be decided". It is submitted that there are, and can be, no hard and fast rules governing the requirements for crystallisation of a "dispute" for the purposes of the HGCRA and so it is a question of fact in each case whether, and to what extent, a dispute has arisen such that it is capable of being properly referred to adjudication for decision.

16–135 It has been said that a dispute is "whatever claims, heads of claim, issues, contentions or causes of action that are then in dispute which a referring party has chosen to crystallise into an adjudication reference".[89] A dispute includes the whole package of arguments advanced and facts relied upon by each side and there must have been an opportunity for the protagonists each to consider the position adopted by the other and to formulate arguments of a reasoned kind in order to crystallise the dispute. Thus, a party cannot in an adjudication abandon wholesale facts previously relied upon, or arguments previously advanced, and contend that because the "claim" remains the same as that made previously, the dispute is the same.[90]

16–136 Where the dispute is to non-payment of monies allegedly due, it is open to the adjudicator to consider any ground that justifies non-payment.[91] This is subject to the limitation that, if the defence relies upon a notice of intention to withhold payment, the adjudicator has no jurisdiction to consider any matter not raised in the notice.[92]

16–137 A question which frequently arises relates to the circumstances in which a responding party may raise a matter by way of defence without having

---

[83] (2001) 3 T.C.L.R. 30; (2002) 80 Con. L.R. 152.
[84] Unreported (July 21, 2001).
[85] Unreported (January 24, 2003).
[86] [2002] B.L.R. 312 at 321–322.
[87] [2003] B.L.R. 316.
[88] Unreported (June 15, 2001).
[89] *Fastrack Contractors Ltd v. Morrison Construction Ltd* [2000] B.L.R. 168 at 176.
[90] *Edmund Nuttall Ltd v. R.G. Carter Ltd* [2002] B.L.R. 312. See also *Fastrack Contractors Ltd v. Morrison Construction Ltd* [2000] B.L.R. 168.
[91] *KNS Industrial Services (Birmingham) Ltd v. Sindall Ltd* (2001) Const. L.J. 170.
[92] *Northern Developments (Cumbria) Ltd v. J & J Nichol* [2000] B.L.R. 158.

served a valid notice of intention to withhold payment. Section 111(2) HGCRA provides that a party ". . .may not withhold payment after the final date for payment of a sum due under the contract. . .". A valid notice is required if the responding party wishes to raise a cross-claim or a set-off.[93] A party who has failed to give a valid section 111(2) notice is nonetheless still entitled to raise before an adjudicator matters of abatement and defence as, for example, whether work claimed has been carried out or whether there is double-counting within the claim.[94] The failure to give notice under sections 110 or 111 "does not relieve the party making the claim of the ordinary burden of showing that he is entitled under the contract to receive the payment he claims. It remains incumbent on the claimant to demonstrate, if the point is in dispute, that the sum claimed is contractually due".[95] However, it also appears that the exclusionary effect of section 111 of the Act extends to cases of abatement,[96] although there are conflicting decisions on this point.[97]

No jurisdiction over an issue. If the adjudicator purports to decide matters **16–138** which, on a true construction of the referral documentation, were not referred to him then the decision is outside his jurisdiction and will not be enforced. In *Bouygues (UK) Limited v. Dahl-Jensen (UK) Limited*,[98] Chadwick L.J. said that the answer to the question whether the adjudicator has jurisdiction depended on whether the adjudicator confined himself to determination of the issues that were put before him by the parties,[99] and:

---

[93] See *VHE Construction plc v. RBSTB Trust Co Ltd* [2000] B.L.R. 187 at 192 where H.H. Judge Hicks Q.C. concluded that the words in s. 111 HGCRA were of ample width to have the effect of excluding set-offs; and *Northern Developments (Cumbria) Ltd v. J & J Nichol* [2000] B.L.R. 158 at 164 where H.H. Judge Bowsher Q.C., relying on the decision in the *VHE* case, went much further and expressed the [*obiter*] view that no deduction can be made after the final date for payment unless the paying party has given notice. And in *Levolux AT Ltd v. Ferson Contractors* [2003] B.L.R. 118, (CA) it was held that where a conflict arose between the obligation to pay the amount stated in the adjudicators decision and the contractual term (payment upon determination) the obligation to pay upon the decision took precedence.

[94] See the discussion of this topic in I.N.D. Wallace Q.C. "The HGCRA : A Critical Lacuna?" (2002) 18 Const. L.J. 117 and "HGCRA Section 111(2) Withholding Notice: "Wrong Answer to Right Question: No Answer?" (2003) Const. L.J. 187. See *Rupert Morgan Building Services (LLC) Ltd. v. Jervis* [2003] EWCA Civ 1563, CA.

[95] See the Scottish decision in *S L Timber v. Carillion* [2001] B.L.R. 516 at 524 affirmed, albeit obiter, in *Watkin Jones & Son v. Lidl UK GmbH (No. 2)* (2002) C.I.L.L. 1847. The Court of Appeal declined to deal with the point in the absence of full argument in *C&B Scene Design Concept Ltd v. Isobars Ltd* [2002] B.L.R. 93.

[96] See *Re: A Company* (1299 of 2001) [2001] C.I.L.L. 1745 and *Whiteways Contractors (Sussex) Ltd v. Impressa Castelli Construction UK Ltd* [2000] C.I.L.L. 1664–1666.

[97] *Woods Hardwick Ltd v. Chiltern Air-Conditioning Ltd* [2001] B.L.R. 23 at 26 where H.H. Judge Thornton Q.C. stated [*obiter*] that an abatement would not be caught by s. 111: *KNS Industrial Services (Birmingham Ltd) v. Sindall Ltd* (2000) 75 Con. L.R. 71.

[98] [2000] B.L.R. 522 at 527.

[99] See the criticism of this approach by I.N.D. Wallace QC, "HGCRA Section 111(2) Withholding Notice: "Wrong Answer to Right Question" No Answer?" (2003) Const. L.J. 187.

". . . If he did so, then the parties are bound by his determination, notwithstanding that he may have fallen into error. As Knox J put it in *Nikko Hotels (UK) Ltd v. MEPC Plc*[1], in the passage cited by Buxton LJ, if the adjudicator has answered the right question in the wrong way, his decision will be binding. If he has answered the wrong question, his decision will be a nullity . . . .".

16–139 **Mistaken answer to an issue.** The Court will not hold that a mistaken answer to an issue, which is within the adjudicator's jurisdiction, is an excess of jurisdiction: *Sherwood & Casson Ltd v. MacKenzie.*[2] In *C&B Scene Concept Design Ltd v. Isobars Ltd*[3] the adjudicator had failed to appreciate that the contractual provisions relating to payment had been superseded by the provisions of the Scheme, so that the adjudicator could be described as having addressed his mind to the wrong question. The Court of Appeal held that the adjudicator had decided the disputes referred to him and, even if he had made errors of law, his decision was binding and enforceable until the matter was corrected in the final determination of the dispute.

16–140 **Breach of natural justice.** Enforcement will be refused where there has been a breach of the principles of natural justice. Paragraph 17 of the Scheme provides that the adjudicator "shall make available . . . . . . any information to be taken in account in reaching his decision"; and a failure by the adjudicator to give the parties a chance to comment upon any material, from whatever source, including the knowledge or experience of the adjudicator himself, to which the adjudicator is minded to attribute significance in reaching his decision, is a breach of natural justice.[4]

16–141 It is not possible to identify all the circumstances which might give rise to such a breach and it is inevitably a question of fact and degree in each case, but it includes: where the adjudicator sought assistance from a programming specialist, but failed to afford the parties an opportunity to comment on the final report prepared by him[5]; a failure by the adjudicator to consult with one party upon submissions made by the other[6]; where the adjudicator fails to make available to one party information he obtained from the other party and various third parties[7]; where the adjudicator uses an

---

[1] [1991] E.G.L.R. 103 at p. 108, letter B.

[2] [2000] C.I.L.L. 1577.

[3] [2002] B.L.R. 93, CA.

[4] para. 17 of the Scheme does not limit this principle, and the principle applies equally when the Scheme does not apply. But *cf. Karl Construction (Scotland) Ltd v. Sweeney Civil Engineering (Scotland) Ltd* 2000 S.C.L.R. 766; 2002 G.W.O. 5–151, in which it was held that there was no breach of natural justice when the adjudicator decided on a basis of law not notified to the parties.

[5] *RSL (South West) Ltd v. Stansell Ltd*, unreported (June 16, 2003).

[6] *Discain Project Services Ltd v. Opecprime Development Ltd* [2000] B.L.R. 402.

[7] *Woods Hardwick Ltd v. Chiltern Air-Conditioning Ltd* [2001] B.L.R. 23.

analysis different to that advanced by the parties[8] without informing the parties of his proposed methodology and seeking their observations on its suitability[9]; where an adjudicator has acted in related disputes arising out of the same project, but between different parties[10]; where the adjudicator held a failed mediation between the parties prior to issuing his decision[11]. Decisions consistently state that the adjudicator must inform the parties of information he obtains from his own knowledge and experience or from other sources and of the conclusions that he may have reached having relied upon those sources. It seems the point or issue in question based upon those sources must have been decisive, or of considerable importance to the outcome, rather than peripheral or irrelevant.[12] It seems probable that if there is a breach of natural justice, the whole decision is unenforceable, and it is not possible to sever the good from the bad.[13] It is not necessarily a breach of natural justice if the adjudicator uses assistants to assist him with his decision, and the analyses behind it.[14]

Breach of human rights.[15] It seems that there is no good defence to **16–142** enforcement by citing Article 6 of the European Convention on Human Rights as applied by the Human Rights Act 1999. Clearly adjudication is a summary procedure using a timetable that may make it inherently unfair. However, it has been held that Article 6 does not apply to adjudication because, an adjudicator exercising functions of the sort required by the 1996 Act is not a public authority.[16] For it to be otherwise, would deprive the Act of effect.[17]

16. CHALLENGING AN ADJUDICATOR'S DECISION

Statutory right. The Act requires that the contract shall provide that the **16–143** decision of the adjudicator is binding until the dispute is finally determined by legal proceedings, by arbitration (where applicable) or by agreement.[18]

---

[8] Which is not in itself objectionable.
[9] *Balfour Beatty Construction Ltd v. Lambeth LBC* [2002] B.L.R. 288.
[10] *Pring & St. Hill Ltd v. C.J. Hafner*, [2002] EWHC 1775 but contrast *R.G. Carter v. Nuttall* [2002] B.L.R. 359, where it was held that no difficulty arose where the same adjudicator was appointed in a number of adjudications between the *same* parties arising out of the same project.
[11] *Glencot Development & Design Ltd v. Ben Barrett & Son Contractors Ltd* [2001] B.L.R. 207.
[12] *Balfour Beatty Construction Ltd v. Lambeth LBC, supra.*
[13] See *RSL (South West) Ltd. v. Stansell Ltd, supra.*, but also see the observations in *Griffin v. Midas Homes Ltd* (2001) 78 Con. L.R. 152.
[14] *Balfour Beatty Construction Ltd v. Lambeth LBC, supra.*
[15] See Sheridan and Helps, "Construction Act Review, Adjudication and Human Rights" (2003) 19 Const. L.J 84.
[16] *Austin Hall Building Ltd v. Buckland Securities Ltd* (2001) B.L.R 272 and see also *Elanay Contracts Ltd v. The Vestry* [2001] B.L.R. 33.
[17] *Elanay Contracts Ltd v. The Vestry* [2001] B.L.R. 33.
[18] s. 108(3) of the Act.

16–144 Effect of the decision.[19] There is conflicting authority as to whether the decision is a cause of action[20] or whether the cause of action is the original claim.[21] It is submitted that there is an express or implied obligation to comply with the decision and this gives rise to a cause of action.[22]

16–145 Procedure for Challenge. The difference between there being a cause of action or not, is that in the proceedings a challenge might be required to the decision rather than a pleading of the issues giving rise to the original liability.[23] The decision of the adjudicator does not affect the burden of proof that otherwise existed.[24]

16–146 The proceedings also raise particular points on costs otherwise not recoverable in the adjudication,[25] whether the decision should affect any application for security for costs[26] and when a cause of action accrues for limitation purposes when an unsuccessful adjudication is commenced just within the limitation period.[27]

---

[19] See Sheridan and Helps, "Construction Act Review,The juridical basis for enforcement of adjudicator's decisions" (2003) 19 Const. L.J. 144.

[20] *VHE Construction Plc v. RBSTB Trust Co.* [2000] 70 Con. L.R. 51.

[21] *Glencot Development v. Ben Barrett* [2001] B.L.R. 207 at para. [33]; *David McLean Housing Ltd v. Swansea Housing Association Ltd* [2002] B.L.R. 125 at para. [14]; *Balfour Beatty v. Lambeth LBC* [2002] B.L.R. 288 at para. [42].

[22] See para. 16–121 above.

[23] See Alexander Nissen, "The Format for litigation and Arbitration after Adjudication" (2003) 19 Const. L.J 179.

[24] *City Inn Ltd v. Shepherd Construction Ltd* [2001] C.I.L.L. 2009.

[25] See *Griffin and Tomlinson v. Midas Homes Ltd.* (2002) 18 Const. L.J. 67 at para. [22].

[26] See Alexander Nissen, "The Format for litigation and Arbitration after Adjudication" (2003) 19 Const. L.J 179 at 184.

[27] *ibid.* at 185.

CHAPTER 17

LITIGATION

1. INTRODUCTION

[Amend note 1: page 538]   **17–01**
Refer to *Civil Procedure 2003 and Blackstone's Civil Practice 2003*.

Paragraph (b): page 538]
replace *"51 Parts"* with *"75 Parts"*.

[Note 5: page 538]
Delete.

3. TECHNOLOGY AND CONSTRUCTION COURT JUDGES

History.

17–02   [Add note 11A: insert note number at end of second sentence: page 539]

11A Now Mr Justice Thayne Forbes.

[Note 15 add at end: page 540]
Assuming an authorised transfer (pursuant to para. 1.3 *ibid.*) a High Court Judge has power to hear TCC business—see *Saunders v. Williams* [2002] B.L.R. 125.

Appeals from TCC judges.

17–05   [Note 26: page 541]
Delete reference to Sched.1, RSC Ord. 58, r.4 and replace with: See now CPR Pt 52.

[Amend text, second sentence: page 541]
Delete "almost".

[Note 27: page 541]
Delete and replace with: "See now CPR r.52.3."

[Delete third sentence to the end of paragraph 17–05 and notes 28–32: page 541]
Replace with "Permission to appeal will only be given where the Court considers the appeal would have a real prospect of success or there is some other compelling reason why the appeal should be heard."[28]

---

[28] See CPR r.42.3(6).

17–06   [Delete text: page 541]
Replace with:"An order giving permission to appeal may limit the issues to be heard and be made subject to conditions.[29] The power to re-open issues upon which permission to appeal has been refused will be exercised only in rare circumstances.[30] Paragraph 4.18 of the Practice Direction provides that where limited permission is granted the Court will either (a) refuse permission on any remaining issues or (b) reserve the question of permission on any remaining issues to the Court hearing the appeal."

---

[29] See CPR Pt 52.3(7).
[30] See *Saunders v. Williams* [2002] B.L.R. 125.

5. STATEMENTS OF CASE

Causes of action.
[Note 56: page 544] 17–12
"(1986) 7 C.L.R. 113" should be "(1987) 7 Con. L.R. 113".

[Add to note 58 at end: page 545]
A fresh cause of action will accrue where further work is carried out which fails to rectify a defect in the original work even though that further work is properly executed. [58A]

[58A] *Alderson v. Beetham Organisation Limited* [2003] B.L.R. 217, CA.

Composite or global claims.
[Add to note 78: page 547]: 17–17
See also the cases of *John Doyle Construction Limited v. Laing Management (Scotland) Limited* [Court of Session—O.H.] [2002] B.L.R. 393 and *John Holland Property Limited v. Hunter Valley Earthmoving* [2003] Const. L.J. 171 (New South Wales).

7. SCOTT SCHEDULE

Form 3. Extras: claim by contractor.
[Correct fourth line: page 557] 17–39C
"Paragraph 0–00" should be "Paragraph 17–27"

8. PREPARATION FOR TRIAL

Experts' evidence.
[Add to note 31: page 560] 17–44
See also *Anglo Group Plc v. Winther Browne & Co Limited* [2000] 72 Con. L.R. 118 for a consideration of the requirement of independence and impartiality in expert witnesses.

[Add to text after note 44: page 562] 17–47B
In a highly contentious matter (or a case concerning allegations of professional negligence) practice suggests that the Court will be reluctant to use its power to appoint a Joint Expert absent consent of both parties.[44A]

[44A] See *Layland v. Fairview New Homes Plc* [2003] B.L.R. 20, which also considers the circumstances in which a party will be permitted to adduce its own expert evidence following the appointment, by the court, of a joint expert.

[Add note 45 at end: page 562]
See also *Britannia Zinc Limited v. Connect South West Limited* [2002] C.I.L.L. 1927.

17–48 [Add to text after note 49: page 563]
The question of admissibility of expert evidence is a two stage considera-tion. The first is whether the evidence comes within the provisions of section 3 of the Civil Evidence Act 1972. The second stage is the nature of the evidence sought to be given.[49A]

[49A] *Liverpool Roman Catholic Arch Diocesan Trust v. David Goldberg Q.C. (No.3)* [2001] B.L.R. 479 where it was held that since the question was one of law, expert evidence would be excluded because that is within the expertise of the Court and further, although the evidence qualified under s.3, the Court would disregard it because the expert was unable to fulfil the role of expert witness due to his close personal relationship with the Defendant.

Documents.
17–50 [Add to note 57 at end: page 563]
and Supplements 1–3

(b) Disclosure and inspection of documents

17–52 [Amend note 60: page 564]
Reference should now be made to *Blackstone's Civil Practice 2003*.

[Note 72: page 565]
Additional citation for *Burrells Wharf Freeholds Ltd v. Galliard Homes Ltd* is "[1999] 33 E.G. 82".

[Add to note 72 at end: page 565]
There is no additional requirement to establish that the initiation of proceedings is itself likely: *Black v. Sumitomo Corporation* [2002] 1 W.L.R. 1562, CA.

Legal professional privilege.
17–53 [Note 76: page 565]
Delete from "CPR r.31.10. . ." to end of note.

(c) Preliminary point

17–57 [Add to note 89 at end: page 567]
For a recent example, with an unsatisfactory outcome, see *Mostcash Plc v. Fluor Limited* [2002] B.L.R. 411.

(e) View

Delay in proceedings.
[Add to note 6 at end: page 569]   **17–61**
See also *Glauser International SA v. Khan t/a Khan Design Consultants* [2002]
B.L.R. 224, CA, where it was held that an overly formulaic approach should
not be adopted since the power to strike out is discretionary and must be
fact specific.

10. SUMMARY JUDGMENT AND INTERIM PAYMENT

Degree of proof required.
[Amend text of second sentence: page 575]   **17–72**
Insert "compelling" between "other reason".

[Add note 44A at the end of the second sentence: page 575]   **17–72A**

44A The word "real" appears to mean that the respondent to the application must have a case
that is more than merely arguable: *International Finance Corporation v. Utexafrican SRPL*
[2001] L.T.L. May 16, 2001, citing *Alpine Bulk Transport Co. v. Saudi Eagle Shipping Co
Inc.* [1986] 2 Lloyd's Rep. 221. The respondent has the burden of proving some real
prospect of success. Although the standard of proof is not high it must carry some degree
of conviction: *Glaxo Group Limited v. Dowelhurst Limited* [1999] All E.R. (D.) 1288. The
proper disposal of an issue under Pt 24 should not involve the Judge in conducting a mini
trial: *Swain v. Hillman* [2001] 1 All E.R. 91.

[Delete last two sentences of text and replace with the following: page 575]
Although it is difficult to envisage circumstances in which a conditional
order will be made, since, by definition, it can only apply where the claim
or defence has a real prospect of success, 24PD.4 appears to contemplate
some intermediate position. This provides that a conditional order may be
made where it appears to the court possible that a claim or defence may
succeed but improbable that it will do so.44B Presumably this may arise
where an improbable factual allegation is made, the truth of which cannot
be determined on an application.

44B A conditional order is one requiring a party to pay a sum into court or to take a specified
step in relation to the claim or the defence and in default the claim or defence will be
struck out. See 24PD.5.2.

Evidence upon an application for summary judgment.
[Delete the last sentence and note 46: page 575]   **17–73**

Stay of execution.
17–75   [Note 50: page 576]
Reference should be to Sched. 1 to the CPR at RSC Ord. 47.

[Note 52: page 576]
See now the notes in Civil Procedure 2003, Vol. 1, at para. 2.4.6.

11. INTEREST

Interest ordinarily awarded.
17–80   [Note 75: page 579]
See now Civil Procedure 2003, Vol. 1, at para. 7.0.4.

Point for award of interest.
17–81   [Add to note 76 at end: page 579]
See also *Kuwait Airways Corporation v. Kuwait Insurance Company (No.3)* [2000] Lloyd's Rep. I.R. 678 and *Quorum AS v. Schramm (Costs)* [2003] 19 Const. L.J. 224.

12. COSTS

17–83A   [Add to note 87A at end: page 580]
See *Dennett v. Railtrack Plc* [2002] 2 All E.R. 850, CA and *Hurst v. Leeming* [2002] EWHC 1051.

Security for costs.
17–84   [Note 90: page 581]
See now Civil Procedure 2003, Vol. 1, para. 25.13.3.

(a) Costs are discretionary

17–88   [Add to note 9 at end: page 583]
The CPR has precipitated a further move towards partial orders for costs which more accurately reflect the degree of success of the receiving party and also an issue based approach: see the commentary to CPR r.44.3.

[Delete note 12 : page 583]
Replace with: See generally CPR Pt 52.

Part 20 party.
17–90   [Add note 17A at the end of text: page 584]

17A See the very wide wording of CPR r. 44.3(1)(a).

(d) Payment into court and offers to settle

[Add to note 28 at end: page 585]   **17–94**
It is unclear what criteria the Court will adopt on an application to
withdraw or reduce: see the apparently different approaches in *Marsh v.
Frenchay Healthcare NHS Trust*, *The Times*, March 13, 2001 and *MRW
Technologies Limtied v. Cecil Holdings Limited*, *The Times*, June 22, 2001 noted
at CPR Pt 36, para. 36.6.2.

Non-disclosure of payment into court.
[Note 41: page 586]   **17–100**
See now Civil Procedure 2003, Vol. 1.

[Note 42: page 586]
See now Civil Procedure 2003, Vol. 1 at para. 25.7.26.

(e) Written offers

[Add to text after third sentence: page 588]   **17–106**
Whilst a Part 36 offer made not less than 21 days before the start of the
trial must be expressed to remain open for acceptance for 21 days from the
date it is made[55A] it may be withdrawn at any time before acceptance since
there is no requirement that the offer must remain open for at least 21
days.[55B] If it is withdrawn it will not have the consequences set out in Part
36.[55C]

[55A] CPR r.36.5(6)(a).
[55B]*Scammell v. Dicker* [2001] 1 W.L.R. 631, CA.
[55C] CPR r.36.5(8).

[Add to note 59: page 588]
The provisions as to costs and interest summarised in the text are designed
to redress any perceived unfairness if there was to be no difference between
acceptance and non-acceptance: *McPhilemy v. Times Newspapers Limited
(No.2)* [2001] 1 W.L.R. 934; [2001] 4 All E.R. 861, CA (paras 19–21).

CHAPTER 18

THE JCT STANDARD FORM OF BUILDING CONTRACT (1998 EDITION)

INTRODUCTION

Amendments to Form.

18–08 [Add to text at the end of the paragraph: page 594]

The 1998 Form has been further amended by Amendment 3 issued in January 2001, Amendment 4 issued in January 2002 and Amendment 5 issued in July 2003.

Amendment 3 was to the following effect:

Item Clause, etc.

1	**22–2**	Additional definitions: "terrorism"; "terrorism cover"
2	**22A**	Additional clauses 22A.5.1 to 22A.5.3; terrorism cover —non-availability—Employer's options; 22A.5.4: premium rate changes—terrorism cover
3	**22B**	Additional clauses 22B.4.1 to 22B.4.3; terrorism cover—existing structures and contents—non-availability—Employer's options
4	**22C**	Additional clauses 22C.1A.1 to 22C.1A.3; terrorism cover—existing structures and contents—non-availability—Employer's options
		Additional clauses 22C.5.1 to 22C.5.3; terrorism cover—non-availability—Employer's options
5	**22B.2**	Local Authorities versions: new text: terrorism cover certificate
6	**22C.3**	Local Authorities versions: new text; terrorism cover certificate
7	**1.3**	Modified definition of "Joint Fire Code"
8	**22FC**	"Joint Fire Code—compliance"—modified provisions
9	**Appendix**	New Entry for clause 22FC.5
10	**31**	Construction Industry Scheme (CIS)—modification of clauses 31.10 and 31.11
11	—	Modifying references to the Standard Method of Measurement

Amendment 4 was as follows:

Item Clauses etc.

1	**25**	Additional Relevant Event—clause 25.4.19 (clause 25.4.20 with CDPS)
2	**26**	Additional loss and expense matter—clause 26.2.11 (Clause 26.2.10 LAXQ)
3	**30**	Private versions only: Amendment to clause 30.2 re. advance payments

Amendment 5 introduces provisions to encourage the use of registered cardholders under the Construction Skills Certification Scheme or equivalent recognised Scheme.

Clause 2: Contractor's obligations

Clause 2.1
[Add to note 37 : page 616]   **18–41.1**
See also Duncan Wallace "RIBA/JCT Final Certificates again", (2002) 18 Const. L.J. 4

Clause 13: Variations and provisional sums

Scheme of Clause
[Add new note 94A after "(clause 13.7)" in line 5: page 658]   **18–134**

94A For a general discussion of the Variation regime, see Ndekugri and Rycroft "Variations under the JCT Contract", (2002) 18 Const. L.J. 310.

Clause 17: Practical Completion and Defects Liability

Damages for breach
[Add at end to note 28: page 676]   **18–183**

A different result appears, however, to have been arrived at in Scotland: see *Michael A Johnston v. W H Brown Construction (Dundee)* [2000] B.L.R. 243.

Clause 18: Partial possession by Employer

Scheme of Clause
[Insert new text at end of first sentence: page 678]   **18–190**
It has been held that a provision such as Clause 18 can operate when possession has been taken of all (as opposed to some only) parts of the works.[32A]

32A *Skanska Construction (Regions) Ltd v. Anglo-Amsterdam* (2002) 84 Con. L.R. 100 at 109.

Use but not possession of part.

18–193 [Add to note 35 at end: page 679]

See also *Impresa Castelli SpA v. Cola Holdings Ltd* [2002] C.I.L.L. 1904

Clause 20: Injury to persons and indemnity to Employer

Clause 20.2.

18–218 [Add to note 56A at end: page 691]

56AA similar result has been arrived at in relation to cl.6.1.2 of the Intermediate Form of Contract 1984 edition: *Scottish and Newcastle plc v. GD Construction (St Albans) Ltd* [2003] B.L.R. 131.

Clauses 22 to 22D: Insurances

18–240A **Amendments.**

[Add new paragraph 18–240A: page 707]

Clause 22 has been significantly amended by Amendment 3 issued in January 2001. In particular, provision is made for the situation where terrorism cover, as defined in the Contract, is withdrawn or discontinued by insurers during the currency of the work. In such a situation, the Employer has the option of determining the employment of the Contractor or of requiring the Contractor to repair loss or damage, due to fire or explosion caused by terrorism, at the Employer's expense. Amendments have also been made to Clause 22 FC (Joint Fire Code—Compliance)

Scheme of Clauses.

18–241 [Add note 68A at end of paragraph: page 708]

Similar, but bespoke, provisions as to insurance were considered by the Court of Appeal in *Skanska Ltd v. Egger (Barony) Ltd.* [2002] B.L.R. 236.

Clause 22A.4

18–244 [Add to text at end of paragraph: page 708]

It has been held that the effect of the contractual scheme is to eliminate the ordinary rules of compensation for negligence and breach of contract so that the building owner could not claim compensation from the contractors but could only require them to carry out reinstatement works and authorise the release of the insurance monies for payment and, similarly, the contractors could not claim compensation from the building owner but could only require that the insurance monies were used for payment of those works.[68A] The House of Lords reached conclusion upon the basis of the following analysis of Clause 22 this A.4:

"The effect of Clause 22A.4. may be summarised in this way. On the one hand there is the position of the Employer. He is not entitled to deduct anything from the sums payable to the contractor under or by virtue of the contract as compensation for any loss and damage which he has sustained due to the fire. This is so even if the fire was caused by the contractor's act or omission or default or by anyone else for whose acts, omissions or defaults he would otherwise be responsible. Clause 22A.4.2 provides that the occurrence of such loss or damage shall be disregarded in computing any amounts payable to the contractor under or by virtue of the contract. On the other hand there is the position of the contractor. Clause 22A.4.3 requires him with due diligence to restore the work that has been damaged by the fire, to replace or repair any site materials that have been lost or damaged by it and to proceed with the carrying out and completion of the works. Clause 22A.4.4 requires him to authorise the insurers to pay all monies that are payable from the insurance in respect of the fire to the Employer, who is required in his turn to use the money for the purpose of paying the contractor and the associated professional fees for the restoration work. Clause 22A.4.5 provides that the contractor is not to be entitled to any payment for the reinstatement work other than the monies received under the insurance policy. As the contractor is entitled to an extension of time under Clause 25, he is not liable to the Employer for losses due to any delay caused by the fire in the completion of the works under the contract." (Lord Hope at para. 47)

[86A] *Co-operative Retail Services Ltd v. Taylor Young Ltd* [2000] B.L.R. 461, CA; [2002] 1 W.L.R. 1419, HL.

Clause 23: Date of possession, completion and postponement

Clause 23.3.

[Add new note 86a after "Practical Completion" in line 2: page 713]   18–262

[86A] For consideration of what amounts to use or occupation, see *Impresa Castelli SpA v. Cola Holdings Ltd* [2002] C.I.L.L. 1904.

Clause 24: Damages for non-completion

Clause 24.2.1.

[Add to note 1: page 718]   18–274

For some assistance as to the type of notice that will satisfy the requirements of clause 24.2.1, see *David McLean Housing v. Swansea Holdings Association Ltd* [2002] B.L.R. 125 at 132—133.

Clause 24.2.1.1.

18–275 [Correct note 2: page 718]
(1987) 39 B.L.R. 30, CA.

[Add new paragraph 18–275A: page 719]

18–275A **Clause 24.2.1.2.** "*. . . deduct from monies due to the Contractor. . .*"
The authorities do not, at present, speak with a certain voice in relation to the question of whether the Employer may deduct liquidated damages from sums due under an Adjudicator's decision. On the one hand, it has been held in relation to a similarly worded provision of the Standard Form of Building Contract with Contractor's Design 1981 edition that the Employer was entitled to deduct liquidated damages.[3A] However, this conclusion has subsequently been disapproved, and the position is unclear until the issue is resolved in the Court of Appeal.[3B] In *Shimizu Europe Ltd v. LBJ Fabrications*,[3C] a main contractor was held to be entitled to issue a withholding notice in respect of an adjudicator's decision where the sub-contract required the submission of an invoice to trigger the obligation to pay.

[3A] *VHE Construction plc v. RBSTB Trust Co Ltd* [2000] B.L.R. 187 at 196–197.
[3B] *David McLean Housing Ltd v. Swansea Housing Association Ltd* [2002] B.L.R. 124 at 131.
[3C] [2003] B.L.R. 381.

Clause 25: Extension of time
[Add new paragraph 18–280A: page 725]

18–280A **Amendments.**
Clause 25 was amended by Amendment 4 issued in January 2002 (Additional Relevant Event—clause 25.4.19)

Clause 25.2.1.1.

18–283 [Add at end to note 10: page 726]
See also *Sindall Ltd v. Solland* (2001) 80 Con. L.R. 152 at 156–157.

Clause 25.3.1.2

18–290 [Add to note 16: page 728]
The Court has held that it is necessary for the Architect to be satisfied that the Relevant Event is likely to cause the completion of the works to be delayed beyond the completion date then fixed: *Royal Brompton Hospital NHS Trust v. Hammond (No.7)* (2000) 76 Con. L.R. 148 at 173.

Clause 25.3.1

18–292 [Amend note 18: page 729]
Amend reference to *Henry Boot* to (1999) 70 Con. L.R. 32: for discussion of cl.25 and concurrent causes, see pp. 37–38. See also *Royal Brompton Hospital NHS Trust v. Hammond (No.7)* (2000) 76 Con. L.R. 148 at 173–174.

Clause 25.3.3
[Insert note 18A after the second sentence of the first paragraph: page 729] **18–293**

18A The requirement to reconsider and deal finally with the question of extension of time within 12 weeks from the date of Practical Completion is directory only and therefore the exercise of this function outside the 12 week period is probably valid and effective. See *Temloc Ltd. v. Errill Properties Ltd.* (1987) 39 B.L.R. 30 at 39.

Clause 25.4.19.
[Add new paragraph 18–315A: page 735]

A new Relevant Event was introduced by Amendment 4, issued in January **18–315A** 2002. This "sweep-up" Event provides for delay due to ". . . any impediment, prevention or default, whether by act or omission, by the Employer or any person for whom the Employer is responsible. . .". The intention is to preserve the Employer's right to claim liquidated damages where there is an act of prevention etc. by the Employer falling outside the provisions of clauses 25.4.1 to 25.4.18. It is thought that the new clause will make it very difficult, it not impossible, to maintain "time at large" arguments under this form of contract since any conceivable act or omission on the part of the Employer is provided for as a ground for extension of time.

Clause 26: Loss and expense caused by matters materially affecting regular progress of the Works

Amendments
[Add new paragraph 18–317A: page 738]

Clause 26 was amended by Amendment 4 issued in January 2002 (Addi- **18–317A** tional loss and expense matter, clause 26.2.11)

Clause 26.1
[Add new note 56a after "reasonably necessary" in line 4: page 740] **18–327**

56A For a Scottish case considering when the limitation period commences in relation to cl. 26, see *Scottish Equitable plc v. Miller Construction Ltd* (2001) 83 Con. L.R. 183.

[Add new paragraph 18–339A: page 743]

Clause 26.2.11
An additional loss and expense matter was introduced by Amendment 4 **18–339A** issued in January 2002. Mirroring the new clause 25.4.19, this matter is concerned with ". . . any impediment, prevention or default, whether by act or omission by the Employer or any person for whom the Employer is

responsible." It is thought that this new clause will now usually make it unnecessary for a Contractor to claim damages under this form of contract and it may be that clause 26.6 is now otiose, at least where the contractor has complied with any relevant notification provisions.

Clause 27.1

18–348   [Add to end of note 41: page 751]
See also for consideration of the very similar determination provisions of Clause 7.2 of the JCT IFC 84 Standard Form of Contract, *Robin Ellis Ltd. v. Vinexsa International Ltd.* [2003] B.L.R. 373.

Clause 30: Certificates and payment

[Add new paragraph 18–399A: page 783]

18–399A   **Clause 30.1.1.3.** "*. . . the Employer shall give a written notice to the Contractor. . .*"
This clause, in compliance with section 110(2) of the 1996 Act, provides for a notice specifying the amount of any payment to be made.[21A] It appears that, if this notice is not given, the amount applied for must be paid.[21B]

[21A] See *VHE Construction PLC v. RBS TB Trust Co Limited* [2002] B.L.R. 187 at 192.
[21B] *Watkins Jones Ltd & Son v. Lidl UK GmbH* (2002) 86 Con. L.R. 155 at 162–163.

Clause 30.1.14.

18–400   [Amend note 21A: page 784]
Amend reference to *VHE* to [2000] B.L.R. 187. See also *Watkins Jones & Son Ltd v. Lidl UK GmbH* (2002) 86 Con. L.R. 155.

Clause 30.6.1

[Add to text at end of paragraph: page 789]

18–419   The Court of Appeal has held that the Architect could not be in breach of his duty to perform his final certifying function unless and until the Contractor had provided him with the necessary documents.[34A]

[34A] *Tameside Metropolitan BC v. Barlow Securities Group Services Ltd* [2001] B.L.R. 113 at 124/125 (a decision on the 1963 Local Authorities Form, but likely to be applicable equally to the 1998 Form).

Clause 30.9.1.1

18–426   [Add to end of note 41: page 790]
See also *London Borough of Hackney & Dagenham v. Terrapin Construction Ltd* [2000] B.L.R. 479, CA.

Clauses 41A-C (and Articles 5, 7A & 7B): Adjudication, Arbitration or Litigation

Scope of Article 5.

[Add to text after the first paragraph: page 862]   18–537

In *R Durtnell & Sons v. Kaduna Ltd*[93A] the Court identified two significant aspects of adjudication under this Form of Contract. The first was that ". . . under clause 41A of the Contract, any number of disparate disputes can simultaneously be the subject of one notice of adjudication" (paragraph 41, page 238). This contractual position is to be contrasted with the position under the Scheme for Construction Contracts pursuant to which only one dispute may be referred to adjudication at a time. However this potential breadth of scope for dispute resolution is somewhat undermined by the Court's other relevant finding as to the relationship between the contractual machinery for extensions of time etc. and the adjudication provisions. As to this relationship, the Court held:

". . . . it cannot be said that there is a 'dispute' as to entitlement to extensions of time, or as to valuation of loss and expense consequent upon a grant of extensions of time, at a time at which the question of whether there should be any extension of time, or any further extension of time has been referred to the architect for the purposes of the Standard Form, the time allowed by the Standard Form for him to make a determination has not expired, and no determination has been made. . . . it is not easy to see how a dispute as to entitlement to an extension of time could arise until that had happened and the architect had made his determination or the time permitted for doing so had expired. The reason is that under the Standard Form it is not for the employer to grant an extension of time or not. That function is entrusted to the architect who is under an obligation to act impartially in making his assessment. Until the architect has made his assessment, or failed to do so within the time permitted by the Standard Form, there is just nothing to argue about, no 'dispute'. Whether the employer is in agreement with a claim to an extension of time is not relevant, because the decision whether one should be granted is not his and he had no role in the making of the decision. He may, under the Standard Form, have imposed upon him an extended contract period about which he is extremely aggrieved. If so, he, like the contractor, can seek to challenge the determination of the architect by reference to adjudication. However, it is between two parties as to a matter entrusted to a third party for independent decision in advance of the decision being known. For practical purposes, therefore, it seems to me that it is a condition precedent to the reference to adjudication of a 'dispute' as to entitlement to an extension of time and as to anything which is dependent upon such a decision, such as a claim for payment of loss and expense in relation to an extension of time claimed but not granted, that the person to whom the making of a decision on the relevant issue is entrusted under the contract between the parties should have made his decision , or the time within which it should have been made has elapsed without a decision being made."[93B]

[93A] [2003] B.L.R. 225. (It should be noted that the Court of Appeal gave permission to appeal in this case but the appeal was subsequently compromised). As to what constitutes a dispute for the purpose of adjudication see para. 16–104.

[93B] para. 42, pp.238–239.

Clause 41A: Adjudication

18–551 [Amend note 12: page 865]

The correct title for the article by K. Franklin is "Beaufort Developments and Amendment 18: the Death Knell for Construction Arbitration?" (1999) 15 Const. L.J. 11.

Clause 41B.4.

18–562 [Add to end of note 21: page 868]

It has also been held that similar wording in the JCT Intermediate Form of Contract is effective to constitute "agreement of all the parties to the proceedings" for the purposes of the Arbitration Act 1996: *Taylor Woodrow Civil Engineering Ltd v. Hutchison IDH Development Ltd* (1998) 75 Con. L.R. 1.

CHAPTER 19

COMMENTARY ON JCT NOMINATED SUB-CONTRACT AGREEMENT NSC/A AND CONDITIONS NSC/C

Amendments.

[Insert at end of the first paragraph: page 896]
    19–03

The 1998 Form has been further amended by Amendment 3 issued in January 2001, Amendment 4 issued in January 2002 and Amendment 5 issued in July 2003. These amendments bring into the sub-contract equivalent provisions to those introduced into the Main Contract by the same numbered amendments: see Chapter 18 above. The subject matter is: Terrorism cover/Joint Fire Code/SMM (Amendment 3), Extensions of Time/Loss and Expense/Advance Payment (Amendment 4) and Construction Skills Certification Scheme (Amendment 5).

SECTION 3

Clause 3.11.

[Add to note 20 at end: page 946]
    19–54

However, the analysis in *Lorne Stewart v. William Sindall* was doubted in *Belgravia Property Ltd v. S & R Ltd* [2001] B.L.R. 424 at 441–442 where it was held, in relation to the JCT Management Contract 1987 edition and following *Gordon Durham & Co v. Haden Young (supra)*, that a name borrowing arrangement did not give rise to a tripartite arbitration agreement and that the claim was a claim under the Main Contract in the name of the Main Contractor.

SECTION 9: SETTLEMENT OF DISPUTES—ADJUDICATION—ARBITRATION—LEGAL PROCEEDINGS

Clause 9B.1.2: Multipartite Arbitrations

[Amend note 33: page 1041]
    19–121

Amend reference to *Redland Aggregates Ltd v. Shephard Hill* to [2000] 1 W.L.R. 1621, HL; see also *Dredging & Construction v. Delta Civil Engineering (No.2)* (2000) 2 T.C.L.R. 438.

CHAPTER 20

THE ICE FORM OF CONTRACT—7TH EDITION 1999

20–02 [Add to end of paragraph 20–02: page 1054]
A third edition of the ICE Conditions of Contract, Minor Works, was issued in April 2001.

20–04 [Add to end of second sentence of the first paragraph: page 1055]
A second edition of the ICE Conditions of Contract, Design and Construct, was issued in September 2001.

An alternative "Term Version" was issued by the CCSJC in September 2002 (1st Edition) together with Guidance Notes. The term version follows the same clause numbering and content of the Measurement Version but provides for work, typically maintenance or remedial work, to be carried out within an agreed term, involving packages of work as required which may be based on re-measurement or a lump sum quotation.

COMMENTARY

Clause 12(1): "*. . . physical conditions. . .*"
20–74 [Add to end of note 60: page 1085]
For a further example of "physical conditions" see *Atlantic Civil Pty v. Water Administration Ministerial Corporation* (1992) 83 B.L.R. 113, High Court NSW.

Clause 19: Generally
20–106 [Insert omitted note 77: page 1098]

---

[77] See para. 10–58.

Clause 19(1): "*. . . all persons entitled to be upon the Site . . .*"
20–107 [Insert omitted note 78: page 1098]

---

[78] See the Occupiers' Liability Act 1984.

Clause 51(3): "*. . . except to the extent that such variation is necessitated by the Contractor's default . . .*"

[Insert omitted notes 80 and 81: page 1150]   **20–240**

---

[80] Particularly by Mr. I.N. Duncan Wallace Q.C., who has incorporated an equivalent provision in the Singapore Institute of Architects (SIA) Form of Building Contract.
[81] *Simplex Concrete Piles v. Borough of St. Pancras* (1958) 14 B.L.R. 80 see also *Howard de Walden Estates v. Costain Management Designs* (1991) 55 B.L.R. 124 and *Shanks & McEwan v. Strathclyde P.O.* (1994) C.I.L.L. 916.

Clause 52: Generally
[Insert omitted note 82: page 1153]   **20–243**

---

[82] Compare cl. 26 of the JCT 1980 Standard Form of Building Contract.

Clause 52(3): Non-agreed valuation
[Insert omitted note 83: page 1154]   **20–245**

---

[83] It has been held that a "fair valuation" may include the Contractor's liability for adverse consequences to a Sub-Contractor: *Tinghamgrange v. Dew Group* (1995) 45 Con. L.R. 105, CA.

[Then add to end of note 83: page 1154]
A fair valuation, in the absence of special circumstances, should include elements of profit and contribution to the fixed or running overheads: *Weldon Plant v. The Commission for the New Towns* [2000] B.L.R 496, a decision under cl. 52(1) of the ICE 6th Edition.

[Insert omitted notes 84 and 85: page 1154]

---

[84] *Wates Construction v. Bredero Fleet* (1993) 63 B.L.R. 128.
[85] See *Mears Construction v. Samuel Williams* (1977) 16 B.L.R. 49; see also cl. 53(1).

[Insert omitted and amended note 86: page 1154]
[1999] B.L.R. 123, H.H. Judge Lloyd Q.C., and [2000] B.L.R. 247, CA.

Clause 52(4): Engineer's power to fix rates
[Insert omitted and amended note 87: page 1154]   **20–247**

---

[87] See *Mitsui v. AG of Hong Kong* (1986) 33 B.L.R. 1, PC, on appeal from (1984) 26 B.L.R. 113.

[Insert omitted note 88: page 1154]

---

⁸⁸ See below.

[Add to the end of note 89: page 1155]
For guidance as to the Engineer's duty to value variations and equivalent duties in relation to cll. 44 (extension of time) and 60(4) (final account) see *Bernhard's Rugby Landscapes v. Stockley Park Consortium* (1998) 14 Const. L.J. 329 at pp.354–364, a case on an amended version of the ICE 5th Edition. A full copy of the judgement of H.H. Judge Lloyd Q.C. is available at *www.courtservice.gov.uk/*

Clause 53(5): Final payment
20–252 [Insert omitted notes 93 and 94: page 1156]

---

⁹³ *i.e.* the Certificate issued under cl. 60(4).
⁹⁴ It may be that this curious feature, which first appeared in the 5ᵗʰ ed., was accidental. It has been corrected in the 4ᵗʰ ed. of the FIDIC Conditions (cl. 53.4) but not in the current edition of the ICE Conditions.

Clause 54(4) to (9): Vesting of goods not on Site
20–256 [Insert omitted notes 96 to 98: page 1160]

---

⁹⁶ The payment is not subject to retention: see cl. 60(2).
⁹⁷ Abolished by the Insolvency Act 1986.
⁹⁸ See *Aluminium Industrie Vaassen v. Romalpa Aluminium* [1976] 1 W.L.R. 676; *Pfeiffer v. Arbuthnot Factors* [1988] 1 W.L.R. 150; *Armour v. Thyssen Edelstahlwerke A.G.* [1991] 2 A.C. 339, HL (Sc.); see also paras. 10–16, 10–17.

Clause 65(2): Completing the Works
20–315 [Add to end of paragraph 20–315: page 1194]
Following the decision of the Court of Appeal in *Cosslett (Contractors) v. Mid Glamorgan C.C.*, proceedings were bought by the Administrator for damages for conversion in respect of the coal-washing plant abandoned by the Contractor. In *Smith (as Administrator of Cosslett Contractors) v. Bridgend County Borough Council* [2002] B.L.R 160, the House of Lords held the employer's right (under cl. 63 of the ICE Conditions, 5th Edition) to sell an asset belonging to the Contractor and to appropriate the proceedings was a floating charge which, being unregistered, was void against the Administrator. Accordingly the Council was liable in conversion.

Clause 66(9): Arbitration

[Add note 60[A] to para. 20–326 after penultimate sentence: page 1201]   **20–326**

[60A] As to the Engineer's decision as condition precedent, see *J. T. Mackley v. Gosport Marina* [2002] B.L.R. 367; [2002] T.C.C.R. 26, a decision under the ICE 6th Edition, following *Harbour and General v. Environment Agency* [1999] B.L.R. 409, CA.

Clause 68(1) (2): Notices to be served on Contractor or Employer.

[Add to beginning of Commentary: page 1205]   **20–339**

For meaning of "principal place of business" see *Van Oord v. Harbour & General*, (unreported), September 2003, *per* H.H. Judge Kirkham.